THE
GOOD LIFE
BLUEPRINT
SERIES

VOLUME 1-3

PATRIK EDBLAD

ISBN: 978-1-950043-06-4

THE GOOD LIFE BLUEPRINT SERIES: VOLUME 1-3

This special collection contains three best-selling books to optimize your life, realize your potential, and maximize your success. Inside, you'll discover:

The Habit Blueprint: 15 Simple Steps to Transform Your Life [page 1]

In this book, you'll learn:

- The neurological loop that drives your behaviors (and how to make it work for you).
- How to get yourself hooked on your habits.
- A simple strategy to make you 2–3 times more likely to follow through every day.
- How to prevent yourself from falling for "mental loopholes".
- How to limit the damage when you have a setback.
- And many more strategies to easily create lasting habits.

The Self-Discipline Blueprint: A Simple Guide to Beat Procrastination, Achieve Your Goals, and Get the Life You Want [page 63]

In this book, you'll learn:

- The four fundamental "keystone habits" of self-discipline.
- How to change your mindset to cultivate success.

- How to establish your mission in life using The Hedgehog Concept.

- How to find your unique "why" using The Golden Circle.

- How to get laser-focused on the right things by defining your Circle of Competence.

- How to biologically reshape your mind and body for success by creating a Winner Effect.

- Several research-backed strategies to radically transform your behavior.

The Decision-Making Blueprint: A Simple Guide to Better Choices in Life and Work [page 197]

In this book, you'll learn:

- The cognitive biases that distort your thinking, and how to counteract them.

- The logical fallacies that derail your judgment, and how to prevent them.

- The mental models you need to equip your mind with to make great decisions.

By the end of the series, you'll know exactly how to build lifelong habits, cultivate relentless self-discipline, and make intelligent decisions. And that will allow you to lead a healthy, wealthy, and happy life.

Let's begin!

BOOK 1

THE HABIT BLUEPRINT

15 SIMPLE STEPS TO
TRANSFORM YOUR LIFE

PATRIK EDBLAD

WHAT OTHERS ARE SAYING ABOUT "THE HABIT BLUEPRINT"

"Many people want to improve their habits, but don't know how to get started. Fortunately, Patrik Edblad provides a simple step-by-step solution for starting (and sticking) to a new routine. It's the perfect resource for anyone who struggles to create lasting change in their lives."

— **Steve Scott, bestselling author of** *Habit Stacking: 97 Small Life Changes That Take Five Minutes or Less*

"Patrik Edblad shows you how to create unbreakable habits without breaking a sweat. When you learn these skills, you'll have the secret sauce to finally follow through on your goals without giving up or getting frustrated. A must-read if you're serious about sustaining habits."

— **Barrie Davenport, bestselling author of** *Sticky Habits: How to Achieve Your Goals without Quitting and Create Unbreakable Habits Starting with Five Minutes a Day*

"I've personally witnessed Patrik lead hundreds of people to complete and total life transformations. This powerful book captures every one of Patrik's habit systems and tricks. With this book in your hand, you will create as many new habits as you can imagine."

— **Tony Stubblebine, founder of award-winning habit tracking app Coach.me**

YOUR FREE GIFTS

As a way of saying thank you for your purchase, I'd like to offer you two complimentary gifts:

1) *The Habit Blueprint Workbook.* We'll be covering a lot of powerful strategies in this book. To make it as easy as possible for you to implement them into your life, I've created a step-by-step checklist you can use every time you get started with a new habit. This resource takes you through all the steps outlined in this book one by one, so you can make sure you put all the strategies to work for you as efficiently as possible.

Go Here to Grab *The Habit Blueprint Workbook*:

https://patrikedblad.com/the-good-life-blueprint-series-bonuses

2) *The Science of Willpower: Proven Strategies to Beat Procrastination & Get Big Things Done.* This e-book will show you:

- Why self-control is so important;
- How willpower works like a muscle;
- Why you should manage your energy, not your time;
- The physiology of self-control;
- Five cornerstone habits of willpower;
- Five powerful tactics to increase your willpower;
- And much more.

Go Here to Grab *The Science of Willpower: Proven Strategies to Beat Procrastination & Get Big Things Done:*

https://patrikedblad.com/the-good-life-blueprint-series-bonuses

CONTENTS

INTRODUCTION

According to research from Duke University[1], somewhere around 40 percent of the actions people perform every day aren't due to decision making but habits.

Take a moment to reflect on what that means. Almost half of the things you do on a given day aren't the result of conscious decisions but behaviors that you have repeated so many times they have become more or less automatic. You no longer think about them, you just do them.

Imagine what it would mean to you if you could find a way to change this 40 percent of actions so that you got them to work for you in every area of your life. What would it mean for your health? Your finances? Your relationships? Your personal growth?

This is why I absolutely love the topic of habits. It's also why I think understanding the mechanics of human behavior is a crucial skill in life. Because when we understand human behavior, it enables us to create our habits, which then create us. Almost every area of life reflects our daily habits:

- How in shape you are is a result of your habits.
- How productive you are is a result of your habits.
- How educated you are is a result of your habits.
- How much money you have is a result of your habits.
- How good your relationships are is a result of your habits.
- How happy you are is a result of your habits.

When we don't have a proper understanding of how habits work, we try to force our way to change by sheer will and usually end up at square one within a matter of months (or days). What's worse, each time we fail, we lose a little bit more confidence and get more and more discouraged until learned helplessness sets in.

If you're at the point where new-year resolutions have become something you keep just for the sake of keeping resolutions, rather than actually going after them, you know exactly what I mean. And you're not alone. About 92 percent of people fail at their resolutions every year[2].

But that also means 8 percent actually follow through on their goals. And contrary to what you might expect, these people are no different from you. They don't possess superhuman levels of self-control and some innate drive that makes them unbeatable.

What separates the habitual achievers from the rest is simply a system they've found to work for them that they use over and over again to create the change they want in all areas of life.

The only thing that stands between you and your most desired goals is really nothing more than a systematic, proven strategy you can use to make them a reality.

This book contains that strategy.

In the next couple of chapters, you'll be guided through a series of scientifically proven techniques for creating habits. Everything will be laid out with very simple, step-by-step explanations and actions based on the latest and best research regarding behavior change.

Sound good? Let's do this thing!

HOW TO USE THIS BOOK

There are two ways you can read this book: passively or actively. Passively means you consume the material, getting a bit of entertainment and learn some new stuff. Reading actively, on the other hand, means you engage with the material, think about how the strategies outlined relate to you, and most importantly, take action on what you learn.

This book contains all the strategies you need to establish new habits and create massive change in your life. But that will only happen if you actually put the tactics to use.

So don't confuse motion with action. Don't settle for just reading passively, nodding along as you go, thinking, "yeah, I should probably do that." Ideas are worthless without execution. So make a commitment right now to experiment with what you're learning. Doing this will not be as comfortable as just reading, but it will make all the difference in how much value you get out of this book.

Since you're the biggest expert in the world on your behavior (and since you likely don't have access to a team of researchers who could do it for you), I encourage you to take on the roles of both scientist and subject from this point forward.

Let life become your experiment and the world your lab.

If you can successfully adopt this "scientist and subject" mindset[3], you'll dramatically increase your chances of creating whatever change you want in your life. Why? Because now, you cannot fail.

Where most people see setbacks as proof of their incompetence and as a sign that they should quit, you'll see valuable data and feedback you can use for your next attempt. Instead of seeing your change as something you have to do, you'll view it as something you want to do. Instead of getting discouraged, you'll get curious. Instead of quitting, you'll persistently refine your approach until you've found a way that works for you.

Sounds good? Are you ready to experiment? Awesome!

I recommend you start by reading through the entire book first. Doing this will give you a good idea of all the strategies and allow your brain to start working on how you could most effectively put them to use. Then download The Habit Blueprint Workbook, pick a habit you'd like to create, and get to work!

Let's get to it!

THE HABIT LOOP

We'll begin by examining how habits work. One very helpful framework for doing this comes from researchers at MIT[4]. They have discovered that all our habits are driven by the same simple neurological loop. This "habit loop" consists of three components:

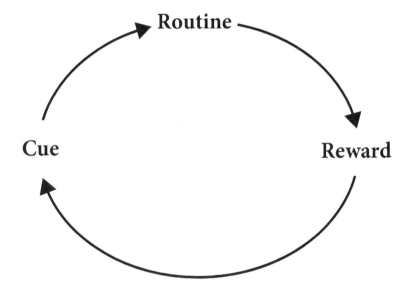

1) A cue, which is the trigger that starts your habit

2) A routine, which is the habit itself

3) A reward, which is the benefit you gain from doing the habit

If you perceive the reward as positive, you'll want to repeat the loop again the next time the same cue shows up. When this sequence gets repeated enough times, it will become automatic and a habit will be formed.

Phone application developers are very aware of this and design their apps in a way that plays right into our psychology to get us hooked on their product.

If you tend to respond immediately to notifications on your phone, you know what I'm talking about. It doesn't matter much what you've got going on at that moment; the urge you get from the notification is enough to make you abort what you're doing and check your phone instead.

Here's how the habit loop works in this scenario: your phone gives off a notification sound (cue), you pick up your phone and check the notification (routine), and get to know what the notification is about (reward).

Knowing that all your habits work this way is very powerful, because it allows you to experiment deliberately with different cues, routines, and rewards until you get them to work for you.

In the next couple of pages, you'll get to learn the best strategies scientists have found for doing just that.

STEP 1: PICK YOUR HABIT

You probably have an idea of the change you want to create in your life. Otherwise, you wouldn't be reading this book. But before definitely deciding what habit to start working on first, I want to share an idea that will greatly enhance the chances for you to get some really explosive results from this book.

Have you ever noticed how some habits tend to "spill over" and create positive effects across all areas of your life? In his book, *The Power of Habit*, author and habit expert Charles Duhigg refers to these behaviors as "keystone habits."[5]

For me, exercise is a huge keystone habit. I know this because whenever I work out regularly, all the other aspects of my life seem to fall naturally into place by themselves: I sleep better, I eat better, I'm way more productive, and I enjoy life more in general.

So, to get a flying start on your habit change, I highly recommend you begin with a keystone habit. Ask yourself what habit seemed to have had this positive ripple effect in your life in the past. It could be exercise, but it could also be practicing meditation, getting proper sleep, decluttering your environment, adjusting your eating and drinking habits, or something else entirely.

If you can think of several keystone habits, that's great, but I encourage you to start working on just one of them the first time you read this book. There's nothing wrong with going after several habits at once, but going through the process with just one habit is very helpful because it keeps things simple and reduces the risk of your becoming overwhelmed.

When you've successfully established one habit, you can then start experimenting with adding several others.

Step 1: Pick Your Habit

1) Reflect on your keystone habits. What behaviors have "spilled over" and created a ripple effect of positive change in all areas of your life in the past?

2) Pick just one habit. This is the habit you will be working on while reading this book for the first time.

STEP 2: START RIDICULOUSLY SMALL

A parole board judge is just about to make a final decision on whether or not to approve a criminal for parole. What do you think will affect this decision the most?

Maybe the crime committed? Or the particular law that was broken? Perhaps the criminal's recent behavior in prison?

These are all reasonable guesses, but as it turns out, they are not even close. No, the most important factor that will decide the outcome for the criminal is instead something as seemingly trivial as the time of day.

More precisely, the chances of getting a favorable ruling will be about 65 percent in the morning and right after lunch. Should the case come up just before lunch or late in the day, the criminal's chances will instead be close to zero.

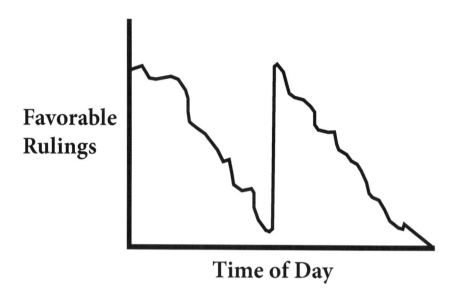

Favorable Rulings

Time of Day

And this isn't true just for some rare, isolated events. The researchers who noticed this trend found that it held true for more than eleven hundred cases, no matter what the crime was.[6] How could this be?

Research has shown that willpower works like a muscle. This idea is known as ego-depletion[7] and explains that just like a physical muscle, your willpower gets increasingly tired the more you put it to use.

You can think of your willpower as a cell phone battery that gets charged when you rest. When you wake up in the morning, your willpower battery will usually be full. As you get out of bed and start your day, your battery level will drop a bit for every decision that you make throughout your day.

And this was what was happening to the parole board judges. As they progressed through their day, making hard decisions about which criminals should get parole and which criminals shouldn't, their willpower became more and more depleted.

The less willpower energy they happened to have at the moment, the less inclined they were to give a favorable ruling. After all, it makes sense to play it safe and keep everyone locked up if you're too tired to make a good decision.

What we can learn from this is that willpower isn't some trait that you either have or don't have. Rather, it's something that fluctuates throughout your day.

So, to ensure that you have sufficient willpower for your habit, it's a good idea to do it at a time when you know that your willpower is high. However, since you can't know for sure that you're always well rested and full of energy, an even better approach is to avoid relying on willpower at all. How?

By starting so ridiculously small that when it's time to do it, it would be silly to say no.[8] This strategy is very powerful because it ensures that your habit won't fail because of random fluctuations in your willpower.

Another benefit of starting really small is it gets you over that initial hurdle of just getting started. You've probably often experienced firsthand that getting started doing something is the hard part. Once you're up and running, it doesn't require much effort at all. For example, getting to the gym can be tough, but once you're there, the actual workout itself usually isn't that bad.

Another benefit you'll notice when using this strategy is that many times, you'll end up doing a lot more than you had initially planned to. For example, if your habit is to read one page in a book, you're likely to end up reading several pages or even the entire chapter. This is because starting small also takes advantage of what psychologists call the Zeigarnik effect, which is our natural tendency to want to finish what we've started and not yet completed.[9]

Step 2: Start Ridiculously Small

Make your habit so tiny that you can easily complete it every day without having to rely on willpower. When I say small, I mean really small. Floss one tooth, do one minute of meditation, take a two-minute walk—you get the idea.

Then, if you feel like doing more once you've completed your small habit on a given day, by all means go ahead and do it. This is the beauty of the Zeigarnik effect.

But whatever you do, do not increase the difficulty of your habit when you're just getting started. No matter what you want this habit to look like down the line, focus on establishing the actual behavior first. If you just stick to the process, your small habit will naturally expand into the bigger behavior with time.

STEP 3: BUILD A CHAIN

When a young comic asked Jerry Seinfeld for advice on how to be a better comic, Seinfeld answered that the way to be a better comic is to create better jokes and the way to create better jokes is to write every day. The young comic recounts Seinfeld's explanation of his system:

> He told me to get a big wall calendar that has a whole year on one page and hang it on a prominent wall. The next step was to get a big red magic marker.

> He said for each day that I do my task of writing, I get to put a big red X over that day. "After a few days you'll have a chain. Just keep at it and the chain will grow longer every day. You'll like seeing that chain, especially when you get a few weeks under your belt. Your only job next is to not break the chain."[10]

This simple strategy is quite brilliant because it plays right into a very interesting aspect of human psychology known in behavioral economics as the sunk cost fallacy. This fallacy can be defined as "the tendency to make decisions about the current situation based on what was previously invested in it."[11]

Here are a few examples to illustrate how this fallacy makes for irrational decisions:

- "I'm full, but I might as well keep eating because I've paid for the food."
- "This movie is terrible, but I might as well watch the whole thing because I've watched an hour of it already."
- "The class is useless, but since I've already paid for it I might as well keep going."

- "I'm going to stay in this bad relationship because I've already invested so much in the other person."

Clearly, the sunk cost fallacy can be a big problem, but we can also get it to work in our favor. And this is precisely where Seinfeld's strategy shines. Every time you put that "big red X" on your calendar, you've invested yet another day into your chain. The longer your chain gets, the harder it will be for you to skip a day as you don't want to lose your investment.

Step 3: Build a Chain

Create a chain-building system. There are two ways you can do this:

1) Get a physical wall calendar. Hang it on a wall where you will see it often and put a pen right next to it so you can easily track your progress every day.

2) Download a habit tracker. If you prefer working digitally, you can download an app that measures your progress. There are plenty of habit-tracking apps out there, but my favorite is Coach.me.

Once you've done this, it's important that each time you complete your habit, you immediately add a new X to your chain. If you stick to this, it likely won't be long before you find yourself pushing through even on uninspired days, just to keep your chain going.

STEP 4: CHOOSE A TRIGGER

Now we get to the first part of the habit loop, which is the trigger that will remind you to initiate the behavior. One of the biggest mistakes people make when they're trying to create a new habit is that they set a very vague intention. Telling yourself, "I should probably work out tomorrow after work" will never create and solidify a big change in your life.

To create a new habit and make it stick, you need to decide on a very specific cue that reminds you to do it, over and over again. The reason creating a very specific trigger for your habit is so useful is that it takes out all the mental effort. Instead of having to think about when, where, why, and if you're going to do the habit on a given day, you just follow a predetermined course of action and get it done without wasting your limited mental energy.

Following are three very effective, science-backed ways to create powerful cues.

1. Implementation Intentions

Professor of psychology Peter Gollwitzer focuses his research on how goals and plans affect cognition, emotion, and behavior. He has found that people who write down exactly when and where they intend to do a certain habit are much more likely to follow through.[12]

This powerful strategy is also deceptively simple. All you do is reframe your goals as "if-then" statements. The "if" represents a situational cue and the "then" is your planned response to that cue. Here are some examples:

- "Journal daily" becomes, "If I'm in bed at night, then I'll write in my journal."
- "Be more patient" becomes, "If I start feeling stressed, then I'll focus on taking three deep breaths."
- "Read more" becomes, "If I sit down on the living room couch, then I'll pick up an awesome book."

To use implementation intention as your cue, you can use either an internal cue (such as a strong feeling) or an external cue (such a particular time, place, object, or person).

2. Habit Stacking

This strategy is similar to implementation intentions, but here you "stack" your new behavior to an already established habit [13]. We're looking to fill in this sentence:

After/Before [established habit], I will [new habit].

For example, you could implement stacking into your daily routines:

- "Before I take my morning shower, I will do five pushups."
- "Before I brush my teeth, I will floss my teeth."
- "After I set my alarm clock, I will meditate for one minute."
- "After I get into bed, I will read two pages in a book."

To use habit stacking write down a list of habits that you do every day without fail. Then go through that list and find the most suitable one to stack your new habit together with.

3. Scheduling

This last technique for creating a habit cue may seem very obvious, yet very few people put it to use. Here's the thing: If you want to make sure something gets done, you put it on your calendar, right? Well, the same goes for a new habit. If your new behavior is truly important to you, it deserves a spot among the other important things in your calendar. Why? There are several reasons:

- It shows that you are serious about this change and that it has just the same priority in your life as, for example, important business meetings. It's a way to tell yourself that you're done dabbling with vague intentions and that you're serious about making this happen.

- We're all susceptible to the "planning fallacy,"[14] a mental bias that makes us underestimate how much time things actually take. When you pre-commit to your habit this way, it forces you to take stock of how much time you actually have for your new habit and reduces the risk overly optimistic planning.

- It eliminates future decisions. Making decisions, even trivial ones, decreases our mental energy.[15] When you commit to a schedule, you free up a lot of mental energy that can be used for more important decisions than whether to do your habit.

To use scheduling as your trigger, get out your calendar and specify exactly when and where your habit will be taking place. If you don't have one, I recommend using Google Calendar and setting a notification for your new habit to make sure you don't miss it.

Step 4: Choose a Trigger

Choose a trigger for your habit using an implementation intention, habit stacking, or scheduling. Which one you choose depends on what habit you're trying to create and what works best for you personally. It's time to put on your white coat and start experimenting. Make your best guess as to which trigger should work best for you and your habit and then start trying it out in the real world. If it works, great! If it doesn't, you can always change it later.

STEP 5: CREATE A REWARD

Now that you've decided on a trigger and the tiny habit that will follow it, it's time to get to work on the last part of the habit loop, which is the reward.

In behavioral theory, reinforcement is "the act of following a response with a reinforcer."[16] This is one of the primary tools in what psychologists refer to as operant conditioning,[17] and it's also what we will be using to automate the habit you're working on so you'll stick to it consistently.

In particular, what we'll be using to do this is our feelings. Now, we all know that our feelings tend to affect the way we act. But did you know that the opposite is also true? Researchers have found that the body language we use, our facial expressions, and even our tone of voice affect our emotions in a big way. Some fascinating studies have shown that:

- By using powerful posture, you increase the dominance hormone testosterone while at the same time decreasing the stress hormone cortisol;[18]

- When you frown for a long time, you're more likely to experience aggressive feelings;[19] and

- Speaking at a lower pitch makes you feel more powerful.[20]

These findings are important, because we can use them to our advantage when establishing new habits. How? By celebrating in a way that stirs up positive emotions immediately after every successful attempt to perform it. When you do this, you get your brain to associate the accomplishment of your habit with feeling good. Your habit becomes reinforced, and you'll be more likely to do it again in the future.

How exactly to celebrate is highly individual and a skill you'll need to practice and experiment with to get good at. (You'll find a list of suggestions at the end of this chapter.) What's important is that you find a way to celebrate that feels authentic to you. If it seems silly, you won't create the positive emotions you need to make the celebration effective.

A lot of people have problems with this step, because they feel like doing such a tiny habit is no real cause for celebration. Stanford University psychologist and behavior expert BJ Fogg suggests you think of it this way:

> The fact that you're learning to change your behavior is a big deal. Think how rare a skill it is. Think how long behavior change has eluded you. And now you are succeeding.

So don't celebrate that one tooth is cleaner. Instead, celebrate that you have taken another step forward to improve your life.[21]

Step 5: Create a Reward

Create your reward. Then use it to celebrate immediately after each successful attempt of completing your habit. You know how often athletes celebrate and how they do it immediately after they've made a great effort? That's what we're looking for here!

Here are some of Fogg's suggestions:

- Do a physical movement signifying victory (pump your fist, clap your hands, or give yourself a thumbs up).
- Yell something out loud ('Awesome job!', 'I rock!' 'Go, me!').

- Vocalize your own fanfare ('Do do do dooo!').

- Imagine a roaring crowd rooting for you.

- Mirror the facial expression of a happy person (smile or laugh). [22]

Of course, these are just suggestions. If you want, you can combine several of them or do something else entirely. If it doesn't feel right to you, keep trying new ways to celebrate until you've found a way that works for you.

STEP 6: SET UP A TOKEN ECONOMY

In his book, The Now Habit, psychologist Neil Fiore writes about how he and his fellow psychology students used to agonize for days over papers that would eventually take less than two hours to write.

It didn't matter how bright they were or how many theories of human behavior they learned. When it came to their own thoughts, feelings, and behavior, they always struggled.

When looking for a solution to this problem, Fiore learned that B. F. Skinner, the founder of modern behaviorism, used a time clock connected to his chair to "punch in" each time he sat down to work.

Whenever he left the chair, the clock would stop, as if here were "punching out". This allowed Skinner to measure his time much like how lawyers and architects do when keeping track of the time to charge their clients.

Skinner then recorded his times in flow charts and awarded himself with a gold star each time he completed a small segment of work.[23]

This strategy of giving out gold stars (or any symbol you see fit) for rewarding and reinforcing good behavior is known in psychology as a token economy.[24] The tokens themselves have no intrinsic value, but can later be exchanged for "backup reinforcers" in the form of actual rewards.

As I've mentioned before, rewarding yourself for good behavior is a crucial part of making it stick, and if we're going to do it, why not use the method the founder of modern behaviorism used for his own work?

Step 6: Set Up a Token Economy

1) Create specific and measurable minimum daily quotas. Before you can reward a step in the right direction, you'll have to determine what that step is exactly and how you're going to measure it. One way to do this that is similar to B. F. Skinner's approach is to use the Pomodoro Technique and give yourself a set number of tokens for each completed twenty-five-minute session.[25]

2) Get some kind of token to reward yourself with. This could be gold stars, coins, poker chips, or something else you happen to have laying around the house. Each time you successfully reach your minimum daily quota, reward yourself with a certain number of tokens. Then start stacking your tokens where you can see them every day to create an inspiring visual representation of your progress that you'll want to keep building every day.

3) Set up your backup reinforcers. These are the rewards you get to exchange your tokens for. The key here is to reward yourself with things that keep you moving toward, and not away from, your long-term goal. In other words, don't celebrate a good week of running by eating chocolate cake but rather by getting a new piece of running equipment. Create a list of backup reinforcers that allows you to progressively build the identity of the person you want to become. For the running example, new equipment and opportunities could be "redeemed" with a certain number of tokens:

   • Water bottle = 5 tokens

   • Running socks = 10 tokens

   • Portable music player = 15 tokens

   • Pedometer = 20 tokens

- Running shoes = 100 tokens
- Entry to marathon = 500 tokens

This is not a perfect token economy by any means, but I'm sure you get the point. What's important is that you create a list of rewards that give you an increasing sense of accomplishment and competence.

STEP 7: SCHEDULE A WEEKLY REVIEW

How long does it take to form a new habit? When it comes to this question, there is a lot of false information out there. One popular estimate that tends to keep coming up is twenty-one days. Another number that's been showing up a lot lately is sixty-six days.

But the truth is, practical as it would be, you simply can't assign a given number of days and expect it to be accurate every time, regardless of who you are, where you are, and what habit you're trying to create. There are just too many variables affecting the outcome for this to be possible.

The "sixty-six days to form a habit" hype mentioned above comes from a 2009 study conducted by researchers at the University College of London.[26] But the specific number of sixty-six days is, unfortunately, a gross oversimplification of the results of the study. What the researchers did find was that it took the participants on average sixty-six days to automate their desired behavior, but for any given person or habit it can take anywhere from 18 to 254 days.

So, if you want to set your expectations right, you should know that it might well take you upward of eight months to build a new behavior that becomes fully automatic. But here's the thing: there's no need to get disheartened by this. Why? Because habits are a process, not an event. This is not something you set out to do for some specific number of days and then forget about. Lasting change never works that way.

Sometimes the habit will feel completely effortless. At other times, it'll be hard work. When you accept this fact and start embracing a longer timeline for your habit, you won't get as bogged down when you run into the setbacks and obstacles that will inevitably show up from time to time.

Instead of worrying about some arbitrary number of days, you're way better off if you create a system that works and then fall in love with the process of consistently executing on that system. In other words, the key to establishing your new habit is to stop obsessing over the results you want and instead start obsessing over showing up every day.

That's the paradox: the moment you stop worrying about the results you want tends to be the moment you can start to make progress toward them. A very effective way to make this shift is to self-monitor your progress,[27] and that's what we'll be focusing on in this step.

Step 7: Schedule a Weekly Review

Schedule ten to fifteen minutes every week to examine the progress you're making on your habit. Ideally, this would be the same time every week. Your weekly review will consist of two simple steps:

1) Celebrate your wins, big or small, and exchange your tokens for rewards.

2) Reflect on the days you missed and adjust your habit so you'll be likelier to succeed next week.

You will learn more about how to adjust your habit in the next couple of pages. But before you keep on reading, get out your calendar and schedule in your weekly review. Make sure you plan it the same way you would with anything important. Because this *is* important, right?

STEP 8: DESIGN YOUR ENVIRONMENT

During the Vietnam War, more than 15 percent of U.S. soldiers developed a heroin addiction. This discovery shocked the American public and President Richard Nixon announced the creation of a new office called the Special Action Office of Drug Abuse Prevention. This office was created to work for prevention and rehabilitation of drug addictions as well as researching and tracking the paths of the addicted soldiers when they returned home. It was this last part, the tracking of returning troops, which led to some fascinating, and surprising, insights.

What the researchers found was that when the soldiers returned home, 95 percent of them kicked their addiction almost overnight![28] This finding was very unexpected as it completely contradicted the usual patterns of addictions at the time. A typical heroin addict would enter a clinic and get clean, but as soon as they returned home, the risk of falling back into addiction was 90 percent or higher. So, the pattern the Vietnam soldiers were displaying were almost the exact opposite. What was the cause of these strange results? In short, their environment.

In Vietnam, the soldiers spent their days in an environment that drove them toward heroin use. They were put under extreme stress, became friends with other soldiers who were heroin users, and the drug was also readily available. Using heroin became their new normal. When the soldiers later returned home, suddenly they found themselves in an entirely different environment. In these surroundings, there weren't any triggers promoting heroin use, and this helped the soldiers drop their addiction.

If you compare this scenario with the situation of a typical drug user, it makes sense that they tend to relapse. The clinic does a good job of removing harmful triggers and makes it easier to get clean, but as soon as this person returns home, all their old triggers will reappear in their environment and make relapse so much more likely. The lesson here is that our surroundings heavily influence our behavior, often without us being consciously aware of it. The triggers in our environment are constantly nudging us one way or another, and we can use this to our advantage.

In his book *Finding Flow*, professor of psychology Mihaly Csikszent- mihalyi writes about what he calls the "activation energy" of habits. The idea is that the bigger the obstacles standing in the way of your desired behavior, the more activation energy you will need to muster up and the less likely you'll be to do it. He explains that "if a person is too tired, anxious, or lacks the discipline to overcome that initial obstacle, he or she will have to settle for something that, although less enjoyable, is more accessible."[29]

So, to make sure your habit gets done, you need to lower the activation energy required to do it. In plain English, this means changing your environment so that your habit becomes easier to do. The more you can lower (or even eliminate) the activation energy needed for your habit, the likelier you'll be to get it done.

Step 8: Design Your Environment

Manipulate your environment in at least one way that decreases the activation energy of your habit. Once you start experimenting with this, you'll probably find that even tiny changes in your surroundings can make a huge difference in your behavior. Here are a few examples of changes to make:

- If you want to read two pages, place the book right where you usually sit.

- If you want to exercise for five minutes in the morning, put your workout clothes next to your bed.

- If you want to meditate for two minutes in the morning, put your meditation cushion in place the night before.

- If you want to eat less, get smaller plates.

- If you want to sleep better, make your bedroom slightly cool and pitch black.

STEP 9: MAKE PROCRASTINATION DIFFICULT

Another study that brilliantly illustrates the power of environment on our behavior was conducted at a hospital in Boston. In this study, researchers secretly manipulated the environment of the hospital cafeteria over a period of six months. While doing this, they ended up helping thousands of people develop healthier eating and drinking habits. How?

At the beginning of the study, the three main refrigerators in the cafeteria were filled with soda. The researchers added water to these fridges and also placed baskets with bottled water throughout the room. The result of these small tweaks in the environment was that in the following three months, soda sales dropped by 11 percent while bottled water sales went up by 26 percent. The researchers also made adjustments in the food options and saw similar results.[30]

Nobody told the cafeteria visitors what to do. The researchers just changed the environment to promote healthier options and the customers adjusted their behaviors accordingly. If your environment supports a healthy behavior, then that's usually what you'll end up doing.

Unfortunately, this is also true for behaviors that we don't want. When we procrastinate, it's very often also just the result of us responding to our environment. If there are snacks on the living room table, we're likely to eat them. If we get an e-mail notification, we're likely to click it. If our phone rings in the middle of creative work, we're likely to drop what we're doing and answer it.

In the last step, you learned how to lower the activation energy of your habit. In this step, your task is to raise the activation energy of competing behaviors. What you're looking to do is make competing, unwanted behaviors harder to do and, as a result, less likely. Take a moment to think about all the behaviors you could end up turning to instead of your habit and then increase the activation energy of these to the point where you won't want to do them.

Step 9: Make Procrastination Difficult

Change your environment in at least one way that makes your unwanted behaviors harder to do. Following are some examples:

- If snoozing is causing you to miss your morning exercise, put the alarm clock in the next room.

- If social media is interrupting your meditation practice, turn off the notifications on your phone.

- If TV is stopping you from reading your book, put the remote control in another room (or put the TV in the garage).

Put the TV in the garage? Yup, I said it. How much you turn up the activation energy of your undesired behaviors is, of course, up to you. But if your new habit is truly important to you, don't be afraid to take some drastic actions regarding your environment to support it.

37

STEP 10: SURROUND YOURSELF
WITH ROLE MODELS

Have you ever noticed how people who spend a lot of time together tend to become more and more alike? Not just in their appearance but in their thoughts, values, and goals. Jim Rohn used to say, "You are the average of the five people you spend the most time with," and contemporary science has shown that there is a lot of truth to this statement.

In a study conducted by psychologist James Shah, college students were interviewed to determine how much their fathers valued high achievement. Shah found that when the students were unconsciously exposed to their fathers' names right before performing a number of difficult tasks, those students who associated their dads with high achievement worked harder and performed better than the other students. This effect was stronger the closer the students reported being to their dads.

Interestingly, when the tasks were completed, they had no idea that they had been working particularly hard. Instead, the inclination to do well was triggered only by unconscious thoughts about their fathers and executed entirely without awareness of this.[31]

And it turns out this works the other way around, too. Unconsciously thinking about someone close to you who does *not* approve of a particular behavior can inhibit you from pursuing it. If your unconscious mind is envisioning your disappointed mother, you'll be less likely to leave dishes in the sink.

Even the goals of people you don't know can have a big impact on what goals you decide to pursue. Psychologists refer to this as goal contagion: our tendency to be more likely to pursue a goal just by seeing someone else doing it.

In one of the first studies of goal contagion, a group of Dutch participants were asked to read a short story about Johan, a college student who was about to go on a vacation with his friends. This story came in two versions.

In the first version, Johan was going to a farm in his village to work for a month before going on the trip. This information implied that Johan had the goal of earning some money to be able to go on his trip. In the second version, Johan was instead going to spend that same month at a community center doing volunteer work.

After reading one of the two stories, the participants got the opportunity to earn some money by completing a computer task as quickly as possible. Those who had read the story where Johan had the goal of making money were 10 percent faster than those who had read the story in which Johan was a volunteer. Without realizing it on a conscious level, the faster participants had been influenced by Johan's contagious goal to make money and had gone after it themselves.[32]

The effect other people's goals have on you can be quite extraordinary. One study found that if you have a friend who becomes obese, your risk of also becoming obese increases by 57 percent—even if your friend lives hundreds of miles away![33]

Without realizing it, we are constantly conforming to the people around us and taking on their goals. That's why it's crucial to surround yourself with positive influences. If you want to create healthy habits but all of your friends are unhealthy, you'll be at a huge disadvantage. If you have big goals you want to achieve in your life but most of the people around you are slackers, you'll always be fighting an uphill battle.

The people you surround yourself with determine what's normal for you. So if you want to get remarkable results, you need remarkable people around you.

Here's probably the most powerful strategy in this entire book: fill your environment with people who are already at the level you want to be (or, at least, are passionately pursuing the same goals as you are) and watch how it transforms everything about you. Before you know it, you'll adapt to the new people around you and unconsciously raise your standards to match what's normal in this new environment. Once you do, it's only a matter of time before you establish any habit you want.

Step 10: Surround Yourself With Role Models

Write down the names of one to five people you know you should be spending more time with. If you can't think of anyone, list out the places, events, or online communities where you could connect with these people. Then take the first step by immediately reaching out to at least one person.

STEP 11: TURN ACCOMPLICES INTO SUPPORTERS

You know how certain people have the ability to light up a room just by walking through the door? And how some other people have the exact opposite effect? Isn't it fascinating how these people can have such a huge impact on the atmosphere in the room just by being present?

Research has shown that this is because of a natural tendency we have to converge emotionally with each other.[34] This tendency is referred to as emotional contagion and happens in an automatic process where we mimic and synchronize the expressions, vocalizations, postures, and movements of the people around us. This, in turn, leads us to "tune in" to the emotions of everyone else.

You might be having a splendid day and feel on top of the world, but if you walk into an environment where everyone else is feeling down, you will inevitably pick up on this and start feeling worse yourself. At the end of the day, your day might well have turned for the worse.

Now think about the implications of this. How does this emotional contagion affect your general quality of life if you spend most (or all of) your time in the presence of negative people? How do you think it affects how you feel and perform every day?

What would it mean to you if you instead were always surrounded with excited, positive, and encouraging people? How would that impact your well-being? What would it mean to always have people to count on for support and encouragement? Just imagine how much this second scenario would do for your performance and overall happiness.

Still, most of us never proactively shape our social surroundings. And that's a shame, because just like the goals of other people affect our behaviors, so do the emotions and attitudes they bring to the relationship.

In the previous chapter, you took the first step to surround yourself with new, positive influences to support your new habit. This step is about changing your already existing social connections. If you have a lot of encouraging people around you, that's great, and we'll get more in-depth about how you can use this more effectively to your advantage in the next couple of pages. But if you happen to have a lot of negative influences around you, now is the time to do something about it by doing either of the following:

1) Turn them into supporters. Explain the role the person is playing in making your change harder for you and then share how you'd like them to help you succeed. A lot of times, a friendly conversation is all that's needed to gain a new supporter.

2) Distance yourself. If someone for some reason can't or won't support your efforts, you need to separate yourself from them. Often, this occurs naturally as you make changes in your life but at times you're going to have to deliberately distance yourself from people who are actively keeping you from creating the change you want.

Step 11: Turn Accomplices into Supporters

Write down a list of one to five people that currently aren't as supportive as you'd like. Then take the first step immediately by reaching out to the first person on your list and ask them to support you in the way you need. If someone isn't willing or able to support you, limit the time you spend with that person as much as you can.

STEP 12: CREATE A COMMITMENT CONTRACT

In a study conducted in the Philippines, researchers had surveyors approach people on the streets with an offer of opening a bank account that paid zero interest. The people who chose to open this type of bank account committed to losing all the money they had deposited if their urine showed any evidence of smoking six months later. So, to recap the offer, that's a bank account with no interest, a good chance of losing your money, plus the discomfort of having to go through a urine test.

Not a very appealing offer, right? Still, more than 10 percent of people approached agreed to sign up for an account. Not a bad turnout for such a poor deal. Even more surprising, though, were the results of the experiment: right around 30 percent of the participants ended up quitting their smoking habit because of it.[35] For this kind of behavior change, that's a huge success rate—higher than is the case with more traditional smoking-cessation aids like nicotine patches.

And when you think about it, it makes sense that this kind of "commitment contract" would be a great motivator to change behavior. To illustrate this, let's have a look at two scenarios:

1) It's 6:00 a.m. on a random Monday morning, and you get brutally interrupted from your deep sleep. While you're fumbling to turn off the alarm, you remember last night's promise to yourself to hit the gym before work.

2) It's 6:00 a.m. on a random Monday morning, and you get brutally interrupted from your deep sleep. While you're fumbling to turn off the alarm, you remember that you have a plane to catch for an important business meeting.

If you're like most people, you'll be much more likely to get out of bed in scenario number two. This is because this situation comes with much greater immediate consequences. We usually don't perceive letting ourselves off the hook for going to the gym as a big deal. We've done it many times before, and the only ones suffering from doing so will be us.

But in the second scenario, the immediate consequences are much greater. Not only does it have a very tangible deadline (the time the gate closes) but you're also financially and emotionally invested. If you don't show up, you'll have to deal with possible financial setbacks and the public embarrassment of letting people down and not sticking to your word.

In the first scenario, it's easy to start rationalizing with yourself about why you need the extra sleep and that it's probably a better idea to exercise after work instead (even though in reality, you very rarely manage to make it to the gym after a long day at work). In the second scenario, all those considerations are off the table. The immediate consequences of staying in bed are simply too high.

This is why using a commitment contract like the researchers offered in the study I mentioned earlier is such a powerful tool for behavior change: it enables you to create self-imposed, immediate consequences for procrastinating.

Let's imagine the first scenario again. Only this time, you remember that you've already committed to following through by promising a friend to meet up at the gym at 7:00 a.m. Or by sending $50 to another friend each time you fail to stick to your workout routine. Or by committing publicly to your family/blog readers/Facebook friends that you will be sticking to your exercise routine for at least thirty days. Or, if necessary, a combination of all of the above. Suddenly, going back to sleep won't seem as appealing anymore.

Step 12: Create a Commitment Contract

Your contract should consist of three parts:

1) Your goal: the habit you want to create. This is where you commit to the tiny daily steps you've decided on earlier in this book.

2) Something at stake: this could be cold, hard cash or your reputation (or a combination of both).

3) A referee: the person who will hold you accountable to your goal. Choose someone who you know will be strict but fair.

Here's an outline you can use:

Commitment Contract

I commit to _____. (For example, "Performing one minute of meditation every day for a month.")

If I don't do this, I will _____. (For example, "Send a friend $50 dollars and/or let my social network know that I failed.")

My referee will be _____. (For example, "A friend who won't have any problems holding me accountable.")

Next, print this contract out and put it somewhere you will see it every day. If you'd prefer a digital alternative, you can use StickK.com. This service lets you create a commitment contract online, and, if you want to raise the stakes even more, donate money to a charity you don't like if you fail. How's that for a clever way to increase the immediate consequences of failing?

STEP 13: GET ACCOUNTABILITY

Back in the 1950s, researcher Henry Landsberger did a study and analysis of data from experiments conducted between 1924 and 1932 at the Hawthorne Works near Chicago by industrial researcher and psychologist Elton Mayo.

The purpose of these tests had initially been to determine whether more light in the building positively affected the productivity of the workers. Mayo did find that the workers increased their output when they were exposed to more light. Interestingly though, they also increased their production when they were exposed to *less* light. What was going on?

As it turned out, it didn't matter what changes the researchers made. The lighting levels or any other variable they would experiment with was irrelevant. As long as they did something, the productivity of the workers would spike.[36]

This tendency would later be named the Hawthorne effect, and the work of Mayo and Landsberger would become foundational in a field in social science known as industrial psychology. What the Hawthorne effect teaches us is that we perform better by the mere fact that we are aware that we are under observation by others.

This is why accountability is such a powerful force when it comes to creating change and establishing new habits. When someone else is tracking your progress and making sure you stick to what you set out to do, you'll be much more likely to follow through.

Step 13: Get Accountability

In the previous step, you created a commitment contract. Now is the time to get it into the hands of at least one other person to hold you accountable. Here are some ideas for how to do this:

- Print it out and give it to your friends.
- Find an accountability partner or group and share it with them.
- Join an online community related to your habit and post it in the forums.
- Send it to a mentor.
- Get a coach and ask for accountability.
- Post it on social media.
- Start a blog and give the URL to a group of supporters.

Don't go it alone. Make sure you have at least one person who is continually following up on your progress and making sure you're sticking to your plan.

STEP 14: PREVENT MENTAL LOOPHOLES

Have you ever noticed how easy it is to fall for the "tomorrow loophole?"

How many times have you told yourself things like:

- "I'm too tired to work out today, and I could always do it tomorrow";
- "I really should stick to my diet, but those cupcakes look awfully delicious. I'll make sure to make up for it tomorrow"; and
- "This project is going to need a lot of work, but I'm sure I can get up earlier and start it tomorrow."

For some reason, we have this highly irrational overconfidence that the things we won't get done right here and now will somehow be easier tomorrow, next week, or even next year.

One study illustrated this tendency perfectly. When the subjects were asked to make a shopping list for what they were going to eat next week, they were inclined to choose a healthy snack over an unhealthy one. Of course, when they were asked what they would choose right now, they were much more likely to choose the unhealthy snack.[37] We want to make the right choice—as long as we don't have to make it right now.

And the tomorrow loophole is just one of the excuses we employ to get off the hook from doing our habit at a given moment. In her book, *Better Than Before*, author Gretchen Rubin lists the most popular loopholes:

- Moral licensing. You give yourself permission to do something "bad" because you've done something "good." For example, "I've been so good at sticking to my diet that I deserve to eat these potato chips."

- False choice. You pose two activities in opposition as if you have to make an either-or decision, even though the two aren't necessarily in conflict. For example, "I've been so busy at work, I haven't been exercising."

- Lack of control. You tell yourself that your lack of control over the situation and circumstances forces you to break your habit. For example, "I'd go for a run right now if I could, but it's raining outside."

- Arranging to fail. Instead of avoiding a temptation, you plan in a way that you succumb. For example, "I'll watch a Youtube video for 10 minutes before I start studying."

- "This doesn't count." You tell yourself that for some reason, this particular circumstance doesn't count. For example, "I'm on vacation, so I'll put off the meditation until I get back."

- Questionable assumption. You make an assumption that negatively influences your habit. For example, "I have to go to work in one hour, and I can't get anything worthwhile done before then."

- Concern for others. You tell yourself that you're acting out of consideration for others. For example, "It would be rude not to drink at my friend's party."

- Fake self-actualization. You accept a failure of your habit by disguising it as an embrace of life. For example, "Why shouldn't I treat myself with this? You only live once!"

- "One-coin." You devalue the meaning of one single attempt. For example, "I can skip the gym today, one workout won't matter."[38]

Step 14: Prevent Mental Loopholes

Reading about these mental loopholes is usually a significant first step because it makes you much more aware of this tendency in yourself. Now, it's all about becoming very skeptical about your brain's rationalizations the moment they show up.

Always remember that you are not your thoughts and that your thoughts are not necessarily right or even looking out for your best long-term interests. Get into the habit of asking, "Is this thought true, or is my brain simply seeking the path of least resistance?"

Create specific if-then "mini actions" to protect your habit from mental loopholes. For example:

- If my brain tries talk to me into staying in bed when the alarm goes off, then I will get up and stay up for ten minutes before deciding whether or not to sleep in.

- If my brain tries to convince me to skip my daily run, then I will put on my shoes and go outside before deciding.

- If my brain tells me I deserve a glass of wine after a stressful day, then I will meditate for ten minutes first.

Pre-committing in this way can be very helpful because it gives cravings some extra time to pass while directing you to healthier and more productive behaviors by default. It can also help you to just get started on the habit, which is usually the hardest part.

STEP 15: PLAN FOR FAILURE

Now, no matter how well you've prepared yourself in the previous steps, it's crucial to realize that there's a good chance you'll still find yourself messing up and breaking your hard-earned chain from time to time. When this happens, you'll likely be very vulnerable to what psychologists have given the catchy name the what-the-hell effect.

One clever study did an excellent job of illustrating how this effect works. The researchers did an experiment in which they asked their participants not to eat beforehand and then treated them all to the same exact size slice of pizza. Some of the participants were dieters and some were not.

After finishing their pizza, participants were all asked to taste and rate some cookies. But the researchers didn't care about how the cookies were rated. Instead, they measured how many of the cookies each participant ended up eating.

That's because the researchers had carried out a little trick: even though all of the participants had been given the same slice of pizza, some of them had been made to believe it looked larger by comparison. This made some of the participants think they had eaten more than they had, even though in reality they had all eaten the same amount.

When the cookies were rated later on, it turned out that the participants who were on a diet and believed they had blown their limit ended up eating more cookies than the people who weren't on a diet. In fact, they ate over 50 percent more! On the other hand, the dieters who thought they were still safely within their limit ate about the same number of cookies as the non-dieters.[39]

I bet there's a good chance you can relate to this tendency when you think back on your attempts to create new habits in your life. In the beginning, it feels great, and you get some nice momentum going. But then, as soon as you miss a day, you're suddenly way more likely to give up on all your efforts entirely.

This is, of course, highly irrational. Just because you miss one attempt doesn't mean all of your previous efforts doesn't count and that you should let them go to waste. Research has shown that missing one single opportunity to perform a behavior doesn't affect the habit formation process in and of itself.[40] This only becomes an obstacle when you let it.

And herein lies the greatest paradox of habit creation. Because, as you may remember from the previous step, one of the mental loopholes, one-coin, means you devalue the importance of a single attempt. And as it turns out, this is absolutely true. If you miss the gym one time, it won't matter much at all. And yet, it will, because it puts you in danger of the what-the-hell effect.

The way to deal with this is to get a bit contradictory in your approach. Defend your chain as if it's super important (because it is), but if you mess up one time, realize that isn't a big deal (because it isn't). Do everything in your power to build as long a chain as possible, but if you find yourself in the situation where you've broken it, simply start a new one right away.

There's no point in ruminating over a missed attempt because stacking guilt and shame on top of what you perceive as a poor performance only makes it harder to get back on track.[41] Let the past be in the past, forgive yourself quickly and get back in the game as fast as you can.

Step 15: Plan for Failure

Decide right now that when you've missed an attempt of completing your daily tiny habit, you will focus on the total number of days you've successfully completed rather than the fact that you've broken your chain. Celebrate what went well, forgive yourself for what didn't, and then get right back into the action.

GRAB YOUR FREE WORKBOOK

And so, we've made it all the way to the end of this book. Great job on reading all the way through! I hope you had a good time, learned what the science of habits has uncovered, and, most importantly, picked up some powerful strategies to try out for yourself.

Because that's what it all comes down to, really. You can read all the books in the world and get fantastic insights and ideas, but they won't create any change unless you actually apply them to your own life.

That's why I encourage you to adopt the "scientist and subject" mindset I wrote about at the very beginning of this book. Try the strategies, view whatever results you get (successful or not) as valuable data, and keep adjusting your approach until you find a way that works for you.

You'll likely find some of the steps in this book very powerful while others are not as helpful. That's perfectly fine and to be expected. While all of the steps in this book are based on successful scientific findings, that doesn't mean they will all fit your unique psychology. Focus on what works and forget about the rest. Or better yet, teach it to others who are struggling with their habits. A strategy that's a complete dud for you can turn out to be very effective for someone else.

Also, remember that this isn't about hitting some arbitrary number of days when your habit will somehow become completely automatic so you can just sit back and slack off. Rather, it's about changing your identity and your mindset in how you approach your life.

Challenge yourself with big, audacious goals but always be very aware that it's your ability to show up every day and take action that will get you there.

They say Rome wasn't built in a day. But they were laying bricks every hour. All you need to worry about is laying that next brick. If you do that, if you can commit to the process and refuse to quit, you will inevitably create any change you want in your life.

Grab Your Free Workbook

If you haven't already, now is the time to download the *The Habit Blueprint Workbook*, pick a habit you'd like to create for yourself, and start working your way through the steps.

https://patrikedblad.com/the-good-life-blueprint-series-bonuses

Oh, and don't hesitate to drop me a message if you have any thoughts, questions, or feedback (or just want to say hi). I love hearing from readers, and I'll get back to you as soon as I can.

Here's to your new habit!

Your friend and habit coach,

SOURCES

1. Neal, David T., Wendy Wood, and Jeffrey M. Quinn. "Habits—A Repeat Performance." *Current Directions in Psychological Science* 15, no. 4 (2006): 198–202. web.archive.org/web/201105261445 03/http:/dornsife.usc.edu/wendywood/research/documents/Ne al.Wood.Quinn.2006.pdf.

2. "New Years Resolutions Statistics." Statistic Brain. Accessed October 12, 2016. www.statisticbrain.com/new-years-resolu tion-statistics/.

3. Patterson, Kerry, Joseph Grenny, David Maxfield, Ron McMillan, and Al Switzler. *Change Anything: The New Science of Personal Success.* New York: Grand Central Publishing, 2011. Kindle edition.

4. Duhigg, Charles. "How Habits Work." Charles Duhigg. Accessed 10/12/2016. charlesduhigg.com/how-habits-work/.

5. Duhigg, Charles. The Power of Habit: Why We Do What We Do in Life. New York: Random House, 2014. Kindle edition.

6. Danziger, Shai, Jonathan Levav, and Liora Avnaim-Pesso. "Extraneous Factors in Judicial Decision." *Proceedings of the National Academy of Sciences of the United States of America* 108, no. 17 (2011): 6889–6892. doi:10.1073/pnas.1018033108.

7. Baumeister, Roy F. "Ego Depletion and Self-Control Failure: An Energy Model of the Self's Executive Function." *Self and Identity* 1 (2002): 129–136. www.communicationcache.com/up loads/1/0/8/8/10887248/ego_depletion_and_self-control_failu re-_an_energy_model_of_the_sels_executive_function.pdf.

8. Babauta, Leo. "The Four Habits that Form Habits." *Zen Habits* (blog). Published February 13, 2013. zenhabits.net/habitses/.

9. Dean, Jeremy. "The Zeigarnik Effect." *PsyBlog* (blog). Published February 8, 2011. www.spring.org.uk/2011/02/the-zeigarnik-ef fect.php.

10. Trapani, Gina. "Jerry Seinfeld's Productivity Secret." Lifehacker. Published July 24, 2007. lifehacker.com/281626/jerry-seinfelds -productivity-secret.

11. Arkes, Hal, and Catherine Blumer. "The Psychology of Sunk Cost." Organizational Behavior and Human Decision Processes 35, no. 1 (1985): 124–140. doi:10.1016/0749-5978(85)90049-4

12. Gollwitzer, Peter M. "Implementation Intentions: Strong Effects of Simple Plans." *American Psychologist* 54, no. 7 (1999): 493–503. www.psych.nyu.edu/gollwitzer/99Goll_ImpInt.pdf.

13. Scott, S. J. *Habit Stacking: 97 Small Life Changes That Take Five Minutes or Less.* N.p.: Oldtown Publishing, 2014.

14. Buehler, Roger, Dale Griffin, and Michael Ross. "Exploring the 'Planning Fallacy': Why People Underestimate Their Task Completion Times." *Journal of Personality and Social Psychology* 67, no. 3 (1994): 366–381. web.mit.edu/curhan/www/docs/Ar ticles/biases/67_J_Personality_and_Social_Psychology_366,_1 994.pdf.

15. Vohs, Kathleen D., Brandon J. Schmeichel, Noelle M. Nelson, Roy F. Baumeister, Jean M. Twenge, Dianne M. Tice. "Making Choices Impairs Subsequent Self-Control: A Limited-Resource Account of Decision Making, Self-Regulation, and Active Initiative." *Journal of Personality and Social Psychology* 94, no. 5 (2008): 883–898. doi:10.1037/0022-3514.94.5.883.

16. Artino, Anthony R. "Self-Reinforcement." In *Encyclopedia of Child Behavior and Development.* Springer US, 2011. Accessed 10/12/2016. doi:10.1007/978-0-387-79061-9_2560.

17. McLeod, Saul. "Skinner – Operant Conditioning." Simply Psychology. Last modified 2015. www.simplypsychology.org /operant-conditioning.html.

18. Carney, Dana R., Amy J. C. Cuddy, and Andy J. Yap. "Power Posing: Brief Nonverbal Displays Affect Neuroendocrine Levels and Risk Tolerance." *Psychological Science* 21, no. 10 (2010): 1363–1368. doi:10.1177/0956797610383437.

19. Marzoli, Daniele, Mariagrazia Custodero, Alessandra Pagliara, and Luca Tommasi. "Sun-Induced Frowning Fosters Aggressive Feelings." *Cognition and Emotion* 27, no. 8 (2013): 1513–1521. dx.doi.org/10.1080/02699931.2013.801338.

20. Stel, Mariëlle, Eric van Dijk, Pamela K. Smith, Wilco W. van Dijk, and Farah M. Djalal. "Lowering the Pitch of Your Voice Makes You Feel More Powerful and Think More Abstractly." *Social Psychological and Personality Science* 3, no. 4 (2012): 497–502. doi:10.1177/1948550611427610.

21. Fogg, BJ. "BJ's Note: September 23, 2012 3:53 pm PST." Welcome to My Sandbox (blog). Published September 23, 2012. tinyhabits.com/sandbox/.

22. Fogg, BJ. "Ways to Celebrate Tiny Successes." SlideShare slideshow. Published August 29, 2012. www.slideshare.net/tin yhabits/dr-bj-fogg-ways-to-celebrate-tiny-successes.

23. Fiore, Neil. *The Now Habit: A Strategic Program for Overcoming Procrastination and Enjoying Guilt-Free Play.* New York: Tarcher-Perigree, 2007. Kindle edition.

24. Ferreri, Summer. "Token Economy." In *Encyclopedia of Autism Spectrum Disorders*. Springer New York, 2013. Accessed 10/12/2016. doi:10.1007/978-1-4419-1698-3_198.

25. Henry, Alan. "Productivity 101: A Primer to the Pomodoro Technique." Lifehacker. Published July 2, 2014. lifehacker.com /productivity-101-a-primer-to-the-pomodoro-technique-159 8992730

26. Lally, Phillippa, Cornelia H. M. van Jaarsveld, Henry W. W. Potts, and Jane Wardle. "How Habits Are Formed: Modelling Habit Formation in the Real World." *European Journal of Social Psychology* 40, no. 6 (2010): 998–1009. doi:10.1002/ejsp.674.

27. Schnoll, Roseanne, and Barry Zimmerman. "Self-Regulation Training Enhances Dietary Self-Efficacy and Dietary Fiber Consumption." *Journal of the American Dietetic Association* 101, no. 9 (2001): 1006–1011. doi:10.1016/S0002-8223(01)00249-8.

28. Robins, Lee N., John E. Helzer, Michie Hesselbrock, and Eric Wish. "Vietnam Veterans Three Years after Vietnam: How Our Study Changed Our View of Heroin." *American Journal on Addictions* 19, no. 3 (2010): 203–211. Doi:10.1111/j.1521-0391 .2010.00046.x.

29. Csikszentmihalyi, Mihaly. *Finding Flow: The Psychology of Engagement with Everyday Life*. New York: Basic Books, 2007. Kindle edition.

30. Thorndike, Anne, Lillian Sonnenberg, Jason Riis, Susan Barra-clough, and Douglas Levey. "A 2-Phase Labeling and Choice Architecture Intervention to Improve Healthy Food and Beverage Choices." *American Journal of Public Health* 102, no. 4 (2012): 584. doi:10.2105/AJPH.2011.300391.

31. Sewell, William H., and Vimal P. Shah. "Parents' Education and Children's Educational Aspirations and Achievements." *American Psychological Review* 33, no. 2 (1968): 191–209. www.ssc.wisc.edu/wlsresearch/publications/files/public/Sewell-Shah_Parents.Education.C.E.A.A.pdf.

32. Aarts, Henk, Peter M. Gollwitzer, and Ran R. Hassin. "Goal Contagion: Perceiving Is for Pursuing." *Journal of Personality and Social Psychology* 87, no. 1 (2004): 23–37. www.goallab.nl/publications/documents/Aarts,%20Gollwitzer,%20Hassin%20(2004)%20-%20goal%20contagion.pdf.

33. Christakis, Nicholas, and James Fowler. "The Spread of Obesity in a Large Social Network Over 32 Years." *New England Journal of Medicine* 357, no. 4 (2007): Epub. doi:10.1056/NEJMsa066082.

34. Doherty, R. William, Lisa Orimoto, Theodore M. Singelis, Elaine Hatfield, and Janine Hebb. "Emotional Contagion: Gender and Occupational Differences." *Psychology of Women Quarterly* 19 (1995): 355–371. www2.hawaii.edu/~elaineh/91.pdf.

35. Giné, Xavier, Dean Karlan, and Jonathan Zinman. "Put Your Money Where Your Butt Is: A Commitment Contract for Smoking Cessation." *American Economic Journal: Applied Economics* 2 (2010): 213–235. karlan.yale.edu/sites/default/files/app2e22e42e213.pdf.

36. McCarney, Rob, James Warner, Steve Iliffe, Robbert van Haselen, Mark Griffin, and Peter Fisher. "The Hawthorne Effect: A Randomised, Controlled Trial." *BMC Medical Research Methodology* 7, no. 30 (2007). doi:10.1186/1471-2288-7-30.

37. Read, Daniel, and Barbara van Leeuwen. "Predicting Hunger: The Effects of Appetite and Delay on Choice." *Organizational*

Behavior and Human Decision Processes 76, no. 2 (1998): 189–205. doi:10.1006/obhd.1998.2803.

38. Rubin, Gretchen. *Better than Before: Mastering the Habits of Our Everyday Lives.* London: Two Roads, 2015. Kindle edition.

39. Polivy, Janet, C. Peter Herman, and Rajbir Deo. "Getting a Bigger Slice of the Pie: Effects on Eating and Emotion in Restrained and Unrestrained Eaters." *Appetite* 55, no. 3 (2010): 426–430. doi:dx.doi.org/10.1016/j.appet.2010.07.015.

40. Lally, van Jaarsveld, Potts, and Wardle. "How Habits Are Formed." *European Journal of Social Psychology* 40, no. 6 (2010): 998–1009. doi:10.1002/ejsp.674.

41. Wohl, Michael J. A., Timothy A. Pychyl, and Shannon H. Bennett. "I Forgive Myself, Now I Can Study: How Self-Forgiveness for Procrastinating Can Reduce Future Procrastination." *Personality and Individual Differences* 48, no. 7 (2010): 803–808. doi: dx.doi.org/10.1016/j.paid.2010.01.029.

BOOK 2

THE SELF-DISCIPLINE BLUEPRINT

A SIMPLE GUIDE TO BEAT PROCRASTINATION, ACHIEVE YOUR GOALS, AND REALIZE YOUR POTENTIAL

PATRIK EDBLAD

YOUR FREE GIFTS

As a way of saying thank you for your purchase, I'd like to offer you two complimentary gifts:

1) *The Self-Discipline Blueprint Workbook.* We'll be covering a lot of powerful strategies in this book. To make it as easy as possible for you to implement them into your life, I've created a step-by-step checklist. This resource takes you through all the steps outlined in this book one by one, so you can make sure you put all the strategies to work for you as efficiently as possible.

Go here to grab *The Self-Discipline Blueprint Workbook*
https://patrikedblad.com/the-good-life-blueprint-series-bonuses

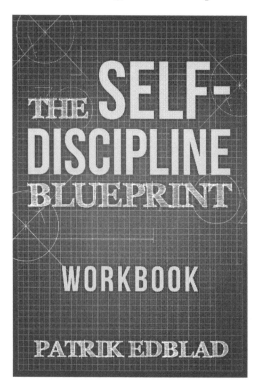

2) *The Science of Willpower: Proven Strategies to Beat Procrastination & Get Big Things Done.* This e-book will show you:

- why self-control is so important;
- how willpower works like a muscle;
- why you should manage your energy, not your time;
- the physiology of self-control;
- five cornerstone habits of willpower;
- five powerful tactics to increase your willpower;
- and much more.

Go here to grab *The Science of Willpower: Proven Strategies to Beat Procrastination & Get Big Things Done*
https://patrikedblad.com/the-good-life-blueprint-series-bonuses

The Science of Willpower:
Proven Strategies to Beat Procrastination
& Get Big Things Done

by Patrik Edblad

CONTENTS

FOREWORD

Our society loves the *myth* of the overnight success. This is the person who achieves amazing success with what appears to be minimal effort.

This myth is so popular because it creates hope. Hope that it can happen to anybody. Hope that you too might strike it rich. And hope that you don't have to work hard to get what you want.

Unfortunately, the reality is *much different* from this myth.

Success is not easy. It usually requires long hours, hard work, and making lots of mistakes along the way. Moreover, if you want to achieve success in any field, you often have to commit to working at it daily.

This means you'll need to build specific habits that separate yourself from everyone else.

And that's why I was excited to read *The Self-Discipline Blueprint* by Patrik Edblad.

There are three reasons why I love this book.

First, Patrik emphasizes the importance of being disciplined enough to form what are called "keystone habits." It's been my experience that success in any endeavor happens when you're willing to *do the same thing every single day*. It might be boring, but it always works!

As Patrik says in his book, "Success almost always requires you to ignore something easy in favor of doing something hard."

Second, I appreciate how Patrik simplified the self-discipline process by *only* recommending four core habits. You've probably heard of these habits before, but do you actually do them every day?

Each of the four habits include many small actions that are incredibly easy to add to your busy schedule. This means you won't feel overwhelmed as you start to become more disciplined.

The third and final reason I like *The Self-Discipline Blueprint* is because of Patrik's idea of "relentless iteration." He feels that you should treat all your goal-achievement efforts as a work in progress. Instead of beating yourself up whenever you experience failure, you should treat these mistakes as a learning opportunity.

The Self-Discipline Blueprint is the kind of book that I wish I read years ago. It's chock-full of actionable advice that you can implement today. I'm confident that in following pages, you will discover a treasure trove of habits that will help you achieve success with any goal.

—Steve Scott, Wall Street Journal Bestselling Author of *Habit Stacking: 127 Small Changes to Improve Your Health, Wealth, and Happiness*

PART 1: INTRODUCTION

The Power of Self-Discipline

Back in 1940, insurance industry executive Albert Gray delivered a speech that has since become very popular.

In his talk, Gray explained that he wanted to find out what makes successful people successful. And he wanted it so badly that he set out on a decade-long quest to find the answer.

He began by reviewing the research on topics like motivation, behavior, performance, and job satisfaction.

Next, he read thousands of books, magazines, and biographies.

And finally, he spent over twenty years conducting empirical research on the subject.

In the end, his conclusion was as simple as it was profound: "The common denominator of success—the secret of success of every person who has ever been successful—lies in the fact that they formed the habit of doing things that failures don't like to do."

The Marshmallow Test

A couple of decades later, in the late 1960s and early 1970s, psychologist Walter Mischel ran a series of experiments.

He and his research team examined children's self-control with a simple test. They began by presenting each preschooler with a plate of treats, such as marshmallows.

Each child was then told that the researcher had to leave the room for a few minutes. Before they left, they gave the child two options: "If you wait until I come back you'll get two marshmallows. If you can't wait, you can ring a bell, and I will come back immediately, but then you can only have the marshmallow in front of you."

As you can imagine, the children responded in a lot of different ways to those instructions. Some kids got up and ate the marshmallow the second the researcher closed the door.

Others did everything they could think of to resist the treat. They wiggled, bounced, and scooted their chairs, but they eventually gave in to temptation.

And, in the end, only a few children managed to wait until the researchers returned with the second marshmallow.

What a Plate of Treats Can Teach Us about Success

The purpose of the experiment wasn't to study the children's strategies to resist marshmallows (although, as you can imagine, it did provide some pretty great entertainment).

It wasn't until years later, when Mischel revisited the children in his study, that he got his results and made a groundbreaking discovery.

When interviewing the participants, who were now in their teens, Mischel and his team found that the kids who had waited longer in the marshmallow test were more likely to have higher grades in school.

Their parents also rated them better at planning, handling stress, having self-control in frustrating situations, and concentrating without getting distracted.

It turned out that Mischel's simple marshmallow test, in many ways, could predict how successful the children would be later in life.

The One Thing Successful People Do Differently

According to Albert Gray, what distinguishes successful people is their ability to do things that others don't like to do.

And that's exactly what separated the participants in Walter Mischel's experiment.

The children who managed to resist the urge to eat their marshmallow—doing what the other kids didn't want to do—ended up more successful.

That is the one thing successful people do differently: they do what they need to do to get the results they want—whether they feel like it or not. And because they consistently do what others don't do, they get results other people don't.

Success Requires Self-Discipline

No matter what you want to achieve, you need to have the ability to be disciplined and take action instead of being distracted and doing what's easy. Success almost always requires you to ignore something easy in favor of doing something hard. And the good news is that if you feel like you're not very good at doing that right now, you can train yourself to become better.

In this book, I'm going to show you how to become more disciplined. I'll lay out all the fundamental habits and strategies you need to develop a strong self-discipline. What you'll discover are the exact same routines and tactics I use every day and that I've used to help hundreds of coaching clients and thousands of readers create the self-discipline they needed to achieve their goals.

I'll take your hand and guide you through everything step-by-step. All you have to do is follow along and implement the action steps at the end of each chapter.

A Good Life Is a Disciplined Life

Now, despite all the talk about success so far, this book is about something deeper.

Imagine for a moment that you were the kind of person who could do what you needed to do, when you needed to do it, whether you felt like it or not. What would it feel like to:

- rise without snoozing in the morning;
- consistently follow the morning routine you've always wanted;
- always be on time;
- begin each workday completing the most difficult task right away;
- eat healthy throughout the day;
- show up at the gym as planned;
- always keep your promises to yourself and the people close to you?

It would feel pretty great, wouldn't it? That's because you, and every other human being, have a need to self-actualize—to express your latent abilities and live your full potential. That's why self-discipline is so critical. Not because it leads to success (although that's a nice side benefit), but because it's a prerequisite for a happy and fulfilling life.

And that's the real benefit you'll get out of this book.

What Others Are Saying about *The Self-Discipline Blueprint*

"In all my life, I've never met someone who is more in tune with the details required to succeed. Patrik's Self-Discipline Blueprint is every step needed for success, tested on hundreds of people and then laid out as a simple path for you to follow to achieve any goal. The secret to success is discipline, and Patrik teaches this better than anyone I know."

—Tony Stubblebine, founder of Coach.me

"This is a concise, well written, and well-organized book. Patrik Edblad not only shows you various important elements that form self-discipline, he also gives you tips how to develop them. His advice is highly practical and applicable, with action steps. I agree with him: success requires self-discipline. This book can help you develop it."

—Joanna Jast, author of *Not Another F-ing Motivation Book: A Pragmatist's Guide to Nailing Your Motivation, Keeping It, and Effortlessly Achieving Your Goals*

"*The Self-Discipline Blueprint* presents no-fluff, honest advice on self-discipline that's easy to implement and adhere to. Patrik Edblad manages to expand upon the fundamental principles of self-discipline—sleep, nutrition, movement, and mindfulness—and make them a natural part of your daily routine. He correctly points out that motivation is too fickle to rely on. If you only take action when you feel a burning desire to it, you won't get too far. He presents the most important steps to acquire self-discipline in fifteen principles in a classic, no-frills style. The main action steps of each chapter are assembled at the end for easy review and reinforcement of the principles covered. He touches on everything from growth mindset

76

and energy management to self-rewards and more with exercises designed to help you understand the material easily."

—Zoe McKey, author of *Rewire Your Habits: Establish Goals, Evolve Your Habits, and Improve Your Relationships, Health, Finances, and Free Time*

"Self-discipline: that thing you wish you had more of but can never seem to call upon when you need to. You're in luck, because Patrik Edblad is here to show you how to find yours. From the basics (yes, you do need to get enough sleep) to more advanced concepts (the circle of competence is your new best friend), you will learn exactly how to show up and get things done. More than that, you'll learn step-by-step instructions for creating an environment where it's hard *not* to get things done. Full of interesting tidbits and absorbing research, *The Self-Discipline Blueprint* is good bedtime reading and even better facing-the-day-like-a-boss reading, so get your copy now!"

—Sarah Beth Moore, author of *Get the Hell Over It: How to Let Go of Fear and Realize Your Creative Dream (Weenie-Proofing the Artistic Brain)*

"Success requires self-discipline. A good life is a disciplined life. I absolutely loved the idea of covering the basics first. Take care of basics; only then can you up your game. If you have troubles with self-discipline, pay utmost attention to this part of the book. There is very little sense in applying advanced techniques if you neglect the basics. *The Self-Discipline Blueprint* is well structured. It contains fifteen strategies to magnify your self-discipline. At the end of each strategy there is a summary and action plan, so you won't be overwhelmed. Use this book as a textbook. Read it once and then study it again.

Pick one strategy, then another one. Implement them and you *will* become more self-disciplined."

—Michal Stawicki, author of *The Art of Persistence: Stop Quitting, Ignore Shiny Objects and Climb Your Way to Success*

"With this power-packed book, Patrik Edblad delivers a complete program for self-mastery and success in all areas of your life. Self-discipline isn't a sexy practice, but Patrik breaks it down in such a way that you actually get excited about tackling the projects and habits you avoid or put off. Clear, concise, and filled with action steps, this book will light a fire under you to become a self-discipline disciple!"

—Barrie Davenport, author of *Sticky Habits: How to Achieve Your Goals without Quitting and Create Unbreakable Habits Starting with Five Minutes a Day*

Let's Get Started!

If you read and implement what you learn in this book, I promise that you'll develop a strong self-discipline.

You'll find yourself taking action when you need to, whether you feel like it or not. You'll do what others don't like to do and get results most people don't. And, most important, you'll experience the fulfillment and happiness that comes from expressing your full potential.

Legendary psychologist Abraham Maslow once said, "If you deliberately plan on being less than you are capable of being, then I warn you that you'll be unhappy for the rest of your life."

So, don't wait. You owe it to yourself to start developing your self-discipline right now.

In the next section, we'll have a quick look at how to best use this book. Then we'll dive right into the good stuff as I lay out the Self-Discipline Blueprint.

Are you ready? Let's do this!

How to Use This Book

The Self-Discipline Blueprint is divided into three parts. Part 1 is the introduction, the section you're reading right now. In part 2, we'll cover the fundamental habits of self-discipline. And finally, in part 3, we'll explore the most powerful strategies you can use to show up and do what you need to do every single day.

As we move on to the chapters ahead, I encourage you to engage with the material actively. Think about how the habits and strategies relate to you and, most important, take action on what you learn. This book contains everything you need to develop a strong self-discipline. But that will only happen if you put the routines and tactics to use.

So, commit right now to start experimenting with what you're learning. Doing that will not be as comfortable as just reading, but it will make all the difference in how much value you get out of this book.

From this point forward, choose to perceive discomfort not as an obstacle but as an opportunity for growth. Imagine that the resistance you experience is a barbell in your mental gym. Each time it shows up, you can either walk away and get weaker or pick it up and get stronger.

Let the discomfort become a trigger for taking action. Face the resistance head on. Again and again and again. If you do that, you'll find that it gets a little bit easier every time you do it. You'll show yourself that you're in charge of your psychology. You'll desensitize yourself to the discomfort. You'll get comfortable being uncomfortable. In short, you'll develop a strong self-discipline.

I recommend you start by reading through the entire book first. That will give you a good idea of the habits and strategies and allow your brain to start working on how best to put them to use. Then download *The Self-Discipline Workbook* and get to work.

Let's get started!

PART 2: SELF-DISCIPLINE HABITS

Master the Fundamentals

Vince Lombardi is considered by many to be one of the best and most successful coaches in the history of American football. In the 1960s, he led his team, the Green Bay Packers, to three straight and five total NFL Championships in seven years. During that time, his team also won the first two Super Bowls following the 1966 and 1967 NFL seasons. Today, Lombardi is part of the Pro Football Hall of Fame, and the Super Bowl's trophy is named in his honor.

Those are some pretty outstanding achievements. So, what was it that made this coach one of the greatest of all time?

"This Is a Football."

In his book *When Pride Still Mattered: A Life Of Vince Lombardi*, author David Maraniss describes what happened when Lombardi walked into his team's training camp in the summer of 1961:

> He took nothing for granted. He began a tradition of starting from scratch, assuming that the players were blank slates who carried over no knowledge from the year before. . . . He began with the most elemental statement of all. "Gentlemen," he said, holding a pigskin in his right hand, "this is a football."

"This is a football." Imagine getting those instructions as a professional football player. You'd probably think to yourself that this coach was nuts. And yet, this methodical focus on the fundamentals was the start of Lombardi's streak as one of the greatest football coaches in history.

And he's not alone. A ruthless focus on the fundamentals has been a recurring theme of many successful coaches. Basketball legend John Wooden, for example, even taught his players how to put on their socks and tie their shoes.

The Four Fundamentals of Self-Discipline

So, what do fundamentals have to do with self-discipline? Well, in one word, everything. There are four foundational habits that everyone needs to feel great and perform at their very best:

1) Sleep
2) Nutrition
3) Movement
4) Mindfulness

If you want to lead a healthy and productive life, you need to master these fundamentals. Take care of them, and you'll approach each day calm, focused, and energized. Neglect them, and you'll be in a, more or less constant state of stress, brain fog, and fatigue.

Upward and Downward Spirals

What's fascinating about your fundamentals is that they are always affecting each other. Depending on how you treat them, they will create upward or downward spirals.

Let's say, for example, that you get an excellent night's sleep. That provides you with enough energy to go to the gym. After you've worked out, you'll want to provide your body with healthy food. That extra energy helps you stick to your meditation practice. And your meditation, in turn, gives you a sense of calm that will improve the quality of your next night's sleep even more.

In contrast, a poor night's sleep might mean you're too tired to hit the gym. Your brain starts craving sugars and stimulants to make up for the lack of sleep and exercise. So, you decide to eat fast food. As a result, your blood sugar spikes and crashes. You don't have the energy to stick to your meditation practice. And, after all that, your sleep is even worse the following night.

If you want to develop a strong self-discipline, mastering these habits is crucial. You can't win basketball championships with your socks and shoes on the wrong way. And you can't win the game of life without your fundamentals correctly in place.

Establish Your Number One "Keystone Habit"

In the next few chapters, we'll cover how to master sleep, nutrition, movement, and meditation. I recommend you start working on just one of them. Ask yourself which one of these habits is your biggest "keystone habit." In other words, which one has had the greatest tendency to "spill over" and create positive ripple effects in your life?

My number one keystone habit is sleep. If I sleep well, all the other fundamentals are much easier to keep in place. But if I've slept poorly, my self-discipline quickly plummets, and I'm not very fun to be around (just ask my girlfriend).

So, getting enough sleep is a big priority of mine. For you, eating well, exercising, or practicing mindfulness might be more important. If that's the case, I recommend you start there. Because once you nail that one big keystone habit, you'll notice that everything else gets so much easier.

You can find all the habits and action steps detailed in this book in *The Self-Discipline Blueprint Workbook*.

Let's begin!

HABIT #1
SLEEP

Dr. James B. Maas is one of the world's leading researchers and educators on sleep. In his book *Power Sleep*, he explains that throughout history, most people slept about ten hours a night. But in 1879, Thomas Edison invented the electric light.

Suddenly, activity was no longer limited to the day's span of natural light, and our sleeping habits started to change. Over the next century, people gradually reduced their sleeping time by 20 percent, to eight hours per night.

But it didn't stop there. Research shows that Americans now average seven hours per night. One-third of the population is sleeping less than six hours per night. As a result, at least 50 percent of the adult population is chronically sleep deprived. And this devastating trend is taking place throughout the industrialized world.

According to Dr. Maas, sleep is not a luxury but a necessity:

> Recent studies of the neurological, chemical, and electrical activity of the sleeping brain . . . show that even minimal sleep loss can have profound detrimental effects on mood, cognition, performance, productivity, communication skills, accident rates, and general health, including the gastrointestinal system, cardiovascular functioning, and our immune systems.

If you want to feel great and perform at your very best, there's no way around it—you need to get sufficient sleep.

How Much Sleep Do You Need?

To answer the question of sleep, we'll begin by having a look at a study conducted by researchers at Washington State University and the University of Pennsylvania. They began their experiment by gathering forty-eight people who were averaging 7–8 hours of sleep per night. These participants were split into four groups:

1) Group 1 had to stay up for three days straight without sleeping.

2) Group 2 slept for four hours per night for two weeks.

3) Group 3 slept for six hours per night for two weeks.

4) Group 4 slept for eight hours per night for two weeks.

All of the subjects were tested for their physical and mental performance throughout the experiment. The participants in group 4, who slept eight hours per night, showed no cognitive decreases, attention lapses, or motor-skill declines. Meanwhile, groups 2 and 3, who slept four and six hours respectively, performed worse with each passing night. Group 2, at four hours of sleep per night, did the worst; but group 3, at six hours per night, didn't do much better. When the study was over, there were two notable findings:

1) **Sleep debt is cumulative.** After one week, 25 percent of the participants of group 3, with six hours of sleep per night, were falling asleep at random times throughout the day. After two weeks, they had the same performance declines as if they had stayed up for two days straight. That's worth repeating: if you sleep for six hours per night for two weeks, your mental and physical performance is just as bad as if you had stayed awake for forty-eight hours straight.

2) **Performance declines go unnoticed.** When the subjects graded themselves, they believed that their performance had

dropped for a few days and then tapered off. But in reality, they were performing worse every day. The takeaway here is that we are very poor judges of our own performance. So, even if you think you're sleeping enough to perform optimally, there's a good chance you're not.

Are You Getting Enough Sleep?

According to James B. Maas, most adults need 7.5–9 hours of sleep per night. If you think that sounds extreme, I'd agree with you. But only because we live in a crazy society. And just because most people don't get enough rest to stay healthy and perform well doesn't mean you have to. As Krishnamurti puts it in *Think on These Things*: "It is no measure of health to be well-adjusted to a profoundly sick society."

To ensure that you're getting enough sleep, answer the following questions:

- How much sleep do you get each night during the week?
- Do you fall asleep the minute your head hits the pillow?
- Do you need an alarm clock to wake up?

If you're sleeping fewer than eight hours per night, if you tend to fall asleep instantly, or if you need an alarm clock to wake you up, you can consider yourself sleep deprived. Other signs of sleep deprivation include struggling to get out of bed; feeling tired, irritable, and stressed during the week; having trouble concentrating or remembering; and falling asleep while watching TV.

You know you're getting sufficient sleep when you feel energetic, wide-awake, and alert all day, without a significant midday drop in alertness. Let's have a look at how to make that happen.

1. Turn Your Bedroom Into a Haven for Sleep

Make sure your environment supports your sleep. Sleep researchers recommend adjusting your bedroom so that it is:

- **Dark.** Light, whether it be sunlight or a lamp, tells your brain that it needs to be awake and inhibits the sleep hormones from being released. So, make your bedroom as dark as you possibly can or get a comfortable sleep mask.

- **Cool.** Most people sleep best in a cool room. The ideal range is usually 65°F–70°F (18°C–21°C). If possible, set your thermostat accordingly.

- **Quiet.** A silent environment is crucial for good sleep. If peace and quiet are hard to come by, you can control the sounds in the bedroom by creating white noise with a fan. Or you can use a good pair of earplugs.

2. Adjust Your Daily Habits

Next, let's have a look at how to sleep better by making a few changes in your daily habits:

- **No caffeine after noon.** Caffeine has a half-life of about 5–8 hours, meaning that if you had a coffee with 200 mg of caffeine in it at 10:00 a.m., 100 mg of that is still in your system as late as 2:00 p.m. So, if you're going to use caffeine, do it as early as possible and preferably no later than noon. If you want to drink coffee later than that, choose decaf.

- **No heavy workouts three hours before bedtime.** Exercise is great for improving your sleep. But not if you do it too close to your bedtime. That's because exercise raises your core temperature when it should be dropping. So, make sure you're not working out too late.

- **No eating three hours before bedtime.** Your body has to work hard to digest your food. Don't make it do that work when it should be shutting down to recover and repair via high-quality sleep.

- **No tobacco.** Tobacco use is linked to an extensive list of health problems, and poor sleep is one of them. How to quit using tobacco is beyond the scope of this book, but Allen Carr's *The Easy Way to Stop Smoking* is a great resource on this topic.

3. Optimize Your Sleep

And finally, here's how to get the most out of your sleep every night:

- **Establish your "Personal Sleep Quotient."** This is essentially how much sleep you need on a given night. Remember that you're likely going to be in the 7.5- to 9-hour range. James B. Maas recommends that you go to bed at a time that will give you eight hours of sleep. If you don't wake up without an alarm and feeling refreshed, give yourself an extra fifteen minutes until you can.

- **Stick to a recurring sleeping pattern.** Once you've established your sleep quotient, be consistent with it. Go to bed at the same time every night and wake up at the same time every morning, including weekends. Of course, you don't have to be perfect, but you'll want to be pretty close. Regularity is important for setting and stabilizing your internal sleep-wake clock.

- **Develop a "pre-sleep" ritual.** To sleep soundly through the night, you need to prepare your body for the long period of inactivity ahead. Use the last hour before bed to find peace and calm. Turn off all your screens (e.g., your TV, computer, and mobile phone) and do something relaxing, like meditation, taking a hot bath, listening to soothing music, light stretching, or reading.

HABIT #1: A QUICK SUMMARY

- If you want to feel great and perform at your very best, you need to get sufficient sleep.

- Sleep debt is cumulative. If you sleep for six hours per night for two weeks, your mental and physical performance is just as bad as if you had stayed awake for forty-eight hours straight.

- Performance declines go unnoticed. Even if you think you're sleeping enough, there's a good chance you're not.

- If you're sleeping fewer than eight hours per night, if you tend to fall asleep instantly, or if you need an alarm clock to wake you up, you can consider yourself sleep deprived.

- Most adults need 7.5–9 hours of sleep per night.

Action Steps

Turn Your Bedroom Into a Haven for Sleep

- ✔ Make it dark.
- ✔ Make it cool.
- ✔ Make it quiet.

Adjust Your Daily Habits

- ✔ No caffeine after noon.
- ✔ No heavy workouts three hours before bedtime.
- ✔ No eating three hours before bedtime.
- ✔ No tobacco.

Optimize Your Sleep

- ✔ Establish your "Personal Sleep Quotient."
- ✔ Stick to a recurring sleeping pattern.
- ✔ Develop a "pre-sleep" ritual.

HABIT #2

NUTRITION

Wouldn't it be nice if you could just go to the store and buy some self-discipline? Well, in a way, you can. Each time you visit the grocery store, you have the opportunity to choose foods that promote health, well-being, and excellent performance.

Healthy foods help you stay alert, energized, and productive throughout the day. Unhealthy foods, on the other hand, have the opposite effects.

And that's why proper nutrition is such a crucial factor in your level of self-discipline. It provides your body with the building blocks and fuel it needs for you to stay healthy and make consistent progress toward your goals.

So, how do you determine what foods to eat?

A Simple Definition of Healthy Eating

There are so many diets out there that it's easy to get overwhelmed and stuck before you even get started. The Mediterranean Diet, the Atkins Diet, the whole-food diet, the Whole30 diet, the Paleo Diet, the vegan diet, the raw food diet, and the low-carb/high-fat diet are just the tip of the iceberg.

With so many options to choose from, how do you know where to start? In my experience, it's best to keep it as simple as possible. A diet is healthy if:

1) It gives your body the nutrients it needs.

2) It does not give your body too many calories.

3) It does not contain a lot of unhealthy stuff, like trans fats and harmful chemicals.

So, a helpful definition to keep in mind is to eat foods with "a good nutrient-to-calorie ratio without a lot of the bad stuff."

A List of Healthy Foods

You have only a few opportunities every day to provide your body with great fuel and strong building blocks. So, don't waste them. Strive to take every chance you get to give your body what it needs. Leo Babauta of *Zen Habits* suggests the following amazingly healthy alternatives:

- **Green leafy vegetables.** These nutrient-dense veggies contain a bunch of great vitamins, minerals, and fibers without a lot of calories or unhealthy stuff. Some examples are broccoli, kale, spinach, bok choy, mustard greens, and romaine lettuce.

- **Colorful vegetables and fruits.** These provide nutrients you won't get much of anywhere else, such as vitamin A, vitamin C, and potassium. Vegetable examples include carrots, squash, and tomatoes. Fruit examples include bananas, oranges, and mangos.

- **Onions and garlic.** These are two of the best and cheapest veggies out there. They protect against inflammation, infections caused by bacteria and viruses (e.g., colds and the flu), cardio-vascular diseases, and cancer.

- **Beans.** Black beans, red beans, white beans, lentils, and peas are all excellent sources of minerals, fiber, and protein.

- **Nuts and seeds.** Walnuts, almonds, cashews, pumpkin seeds, and chia seeds contain tons of protein and healthy fats.

- **Proteins.** Meat eaters can get their protein from fish and poultry. Red meat—for example, sausage, bacon, corned beef, steak, and hamburger—should be consumed in moderation as it's been shown to increase the risk of cancer. Vegetarians and vegans can get their protein from vegetables, whole grains, tofu, tempeh, seitan, and nondairy milks like almond, cashew, hemp, and soy.

- **Fats.** Polyunsaturated fats are especially healthy and seem to lower risks of cancer and cardiovascular diseases. Examples include avocados, walnuts, sunflower seeds, olive oil, fish, and soybeans.

- **Drinks.** Water is best, but black coffee, tea, and green juice are great, too. You should try to avoid drinking sugary drinks and too much alcohol.

Take a Gradual Approach

It can be tempting to try to overhaul your diet overnight, but if you've tried that in the past, you know how difficult it can be. It quickly becomes a lot of work to learn a bunch of new recipes. Social situations become an issue as you're unsure what to eat when you go out. Soon, you'll start getting overwhelmed and begin to miss your old diet. And before you know it, you're back where you started.

To avoid that scenario, I highly recommend a gradual approach. Instead of creating a big, abrupt change in your diet, make just one small change every week. That will help you transition much more smoothly into your new diet. You'll be a lot less overwhelmed and have a lot more fun doing it. Here are some examples of gradual changes to make:

- Have a piece of fruit with breakfast.
- Remove sugar from your coffee.
- Add a vegetable to your lunch every day.
- Switch to a healthy dessert, like a small square of dark chocolate or some maple syrup–glazed walnuts.
- Eat fruit for an afternoon snack.
- Add a vegetable to your dinner every day.
- Don't eat after 8:00 p.m.
- Cut back on one alcoholic drink at night.
- Learn one new healthy recipe.
- Prepare weekday lunches on Sundays.

You get the idea. Keep making small changes like these every week, and you'll be surprised at how quickly you'll transition into a healthy diet.

Nudge Yourself Toward Healthy Eating

Another powerful strategy for changing your diet is to change your environment. In his book *Mindless Eating*, Cornell University professor Brian Wansink recommends the following strategies:

- **Use small plates.** Big plates mean big servings. And that means you eat more. If you start serving your dinner on 10-inch plates instead of 12-inch plates, you'll eat 22 percent less food over the course of a year. So, if you want to eat less, smaller plates are a great investment.

- **Use tall and slender glasses.** Our brains tend to perceive taller drinks as bigger than round, wide mugs. And that makes us drink less from taller glasses. In fact, you will drink about 20 percent less from a tall, slender glass than you would from a short, fat glass.

- **Put healthy snacks in prominent places.** For example, you could put a bowl of nuts or fruit near the front door of your house. That will make you much more likely to grab a healthy snack when you're leaving the house.

- **Hide unhealthy foods and let healthy ones show.** Wrap unhealthy food in tinfoil and store it behind other stuff in the fridge. Wrap healthy food in plastic wrap and store it at the front of the shelf. That will nudge you toward healthier choices.

By proactively making changes like these to your environment, you can nudge yourself toward healthier eating decisions. And, as a result, there's a good chance you'll improve your diet without even noticing it.

HABIT #2: A QUICK SUMMARY

- Each time you visit the grocery store, you have the opportunity to choose foods that promote health, well-being, and excellent performance.

- A helpful definition to keep in mind is to eat foods with "a good nutrient-to-calorie ratio without a lot of bad the stuff."

- Take every chance you get to provide your body with nutritious foods.

- Instead of creating a big, abrupt change in your diet, make just one small change every week.

- Nudge yourself toward healthy eating habits by changing your environment.

Action Steps

Choose Healthy Foods

✔ Base your diet on foods with "a good nutrient-to-calorie ratio without a lot of the bad stuff."

Take a Gradual Approach

✔ Make just one small dietary change each week.

Nudge Yourself Toward Healthy Eating

✔ Shape your environment so that it supports the eating behaviors you want to practice.

HABIT #3
MOVEMENT

Ever since the dawn of humanity, we've been hunting and gathering, dancing around the fire, walking, running, jumping, climbing, crawling, lifting, swimming, fighting, and having sex. The demands of all these movements have shaped us from head to toe.

In her book *Move Your DNA*, biomechanist Katy Bowman explains that there are more than one trillion cells in your body. Almost every one of them has unique equipment specialized to detect your movement. And just as diet, stress, and environmental factors can change the expression (or the physical outcome) of your DNA, so can physical activity.

That is why movement is one of our fundamental habits. Every single thing our bodies do needs movement to work optimally. Functions like immunity, reproduction, and digestion all require us to move. If we don't, it doesn't matter if we sleep sufficiently and eat a healthy diet. Without the loads created by physical activity, these efforts will be thwarted at a cellular level, and we won't function optimally.

Movement versus Exercise

There's a difference between exercise and movement. Weight lifting, trail running, and swimming are examples of exercise. Walking to the store, taking the stairs, and stretching your back are examples of movement. Both exercise and movement may use your body in similar ways, but to give your body what it needs, it's still important to understand the difference. You can think of it this way: movement transcends and includes exercise.

The reason this is such a crucial distinction to understand is that we can be active *and* sedentary. Even if you dutifully show up at the gym every week, your body will still suffer if you spend the rest of the day sitting. Research has shown that people who spend a lot of time sitting are significantly more likely to die prematurely—regardless if they exercise or not.

Exercise is important, but we also need to move a lot more. How much more? Well, here's the thing: these days, most people would be proud if they managed to exercise five hours a week. But that's not even close to our hunter-gatherer ancestors. They would move up to eight hours *a day*. And even when they were resting, it was an active kind of rest. They were constantly "on their toes" and ready to move.

Now, the good news is you don't have to sell your stuff and head off to some cave to be able to move all day. A few small changes in your daily choices can have an enormous impact on your health and vitality. And that's not all.

The Benefits of Movement

These days, it's common knowledge that physical activity can help us lose weight, combat diseases, and boost our energy. But there are plenty of other benefits. In his book *Spark*, neuropsychiatry expert John Ratey explains:

> Physical activity sparks biological changes that encourage brain cells to bind to one another. For the brain to learn, these connections must be made; they reflect the brain's fundamental ability to adapt to challenges. The more neuroscientists discover about this process, the clearer it becomes that exercise provides an unparalleled stimulus, creating an environment in which the brain is ready, willing, and able to learn.

That's because movement stimulates the release of positive neurotransmitters, like dopamine (which encourages motivation, attention, and pleasure), serotonin (which enhances learning, mood, and self-esteem), and norepinephrine (which leads to arousal and alertness). And, most important, movement increases the production of BDNF, a protein which Ratey has dubbed "Miracle-Gro for the brain":

> Researchers found that if they sprinkled BDNF onto neurons in a petri dish, the cells automatically sprouted new branches, producing the same structural growth required for learning.

So, movement is just as important for the functioning of the brain as it is for the rest of the body. All in all, it's crucial for our well-being and performance. Oh, and for the particular purpose of this book, you might also want to know that it can be a tremendous self-discipline booster. Research has found that two months of exercise can be enough to significantly increase the ability to resist temptation and persevere in challenging situations.

Those are some pretty sweet benefits, don't you think? So, how do you make exercise and movement regular parts of your daily routine?

Find Your OTMs

At first glance, making time for daily movement might seem difficult. But it doesn't have to be. In her book, *No Sweat*, motivation scientist Michelle Segar writes that it can be a lot of fun to find what she calls your OTMs—opportunities to move. When you start looking for them, you'll be amazed at how often you become aware of free spaces in the day that are perfect for movement.

A handy framework for finding your OTMs is to divide them into what philosopher Brian Johnson refers to as micro, mini, and macro movements:

- **Micro movements are simple shifts from static to dynamic.** For example, stretching every time you open your email, taking the stairs instead of the elevator, or changing your sitting position every fifteen minutes.

- **Mini movements are slightly longer dynamic movements.** For example, doing a sun salutation every morning, doing five pushups during each break throughout the day, or walking five thousand steps every day.

- **Macro movements are typical exercise sessions.** For example, running, dancing, weight lifting, and doing tai chi or yoga.

By regularly engaging in all these kinds of movement, you optimize your daily routine for physical activity and limit the time spent sedentary every day. I recommend you start by picking one micro, one mini, and one macro movement to implement first. For example:

- back stretches (micro movement);
- sun salutation (mini movement); and
- running (macro movement).

Then use the following strategies to make each type of movement a part of your routine.

Create Triggers

Until your movements have become habitual, you're going to need cues that remind you to do them. The best way of doing that is to create if-then plans for all of them. For example:

- **Micro movement:** *If* I open my email, *then* I will stretch my back.
- **Mini movement:** *If* I get out of bed in the morning, *then* I will do a sun salutation.
- **Macro movement:** *If* I leave the office on a Monday, Wednesday, or Friday, *then* I will go running.

Design Your Environment

Make sure that your surroundings are designed in a way that nudges you to move without thinking about it. You can, for example:

- get a parking space farther away from the office;

- place your wastebasket across the room;

- get a standing desk;

- put your phone someplace where you'll have to get up to answer it;

- do "walk and talks" instead of meetings in which everyone is sitting down.

Make It a Game

Each time you finish a micro, mini, and macro movement, write it down in a calendar. At the end of the day, count your movements and see how that day compares to previous days. Keep adding new movements and compete with yourself to move a little more every week.

HABIT #3: A QUICK SUMMARY

- There are more than one trillion cells in your body. And almost every one of them has unique equipment specializing in movement.

- Your body was designed for movement. If it doesn't get to do that, it won't function optimally.

- You can be active *and* sedentary. Even if you dutifully show up at the gym every week, your body will suffer if you spend the rest of your days sitting.

- You need both exercise and movement. Exercise includes things like running, yoga, or strength training. Movement includes getting up from your desk, stretching, and walking to the store.

- Physical activity is crucial not only for your health but also for the functioning of your brain and the strength of your self-discipline.

Action Steps

Find Your OTMs

✔ Establish your micro, mini, and macro movements.

Create Triggers

✔ Use if-then plans to remind you to do your movements.

Design Your Environment

✔ Shape your surroundings so they nudge you to move without thinking about it.

Make It a Game

✔ Track your movements, compete with yourself, and try to move a little more every week.

HABIT #4

MINDFULNESS

Let's try a little experiment right now. Finish this paragraph, then close your eyes for thirty seconds. During that time, try to think about absolutely nothing. Are you ready? Go!

My guess is that wasn't very easy. Most likely, a variety of random thoughts popped into your head. Maybe you thought about an assignment that's due tomorrow. Or a movie you saw recently. Or an argument you had with a friend.

If you've ever tried meditation, you're familiar with the experience you just had. You closed your eyes and tried to silence your mind, even for just a few seconds, but thoughts still kept popping up.

Zen Buddhism teachers talk a lot about this "mind chatter" you just witnessed. And the thing about that mind chatter is that it never stops.

By practicing techniques like mindfulness meditation, you can learn to quiet your mind chatter. And while that is certainly useful, it also has another significant benefit. That benefit is the ability to differentiate between the "two minds." Let me explain.

The Thinking Mind and the Observing Mind

When you close your eyes and try to think of nothing and thoughts still keep popping up, obviously your mind is thinking.

But have you ever asked yourself this: "If my mind is thinking, then who is observing my mind thinking?"

It's weird, isn't it?

When you did the exercise at the beginning of this chapter, and your mind kept returning to your assignment at work, who was it that was watching your mind worry about work?

It was your mind watching your mind.

In Zen, this is referred to as the two minds—the "thinking mind" and the "observing mind."

This idea has been around for centuries in Buddhism, and contemporary therapies like acceptance and commitment therapy are beginning to implement it after realizing how useful it is for solving everyday emotional problems.

An Intrusive White Bear

The problem with the thinking mind is that you can't completely control it. To prove that point, let's do another quick experiment. Once again, finish this paragraph, then close your eyes for thirty seconds. This time, you can think about whatever you want—except a white bear. Are you ready? Go!

Now, not only did you think about a white bear. You were also *watching yourself* think about a white bear. Your observing mind was watching your thinking mind produce thoughts and images of the bear. It didn't matter that you didn't want to do it. In fact, the more you tried to suppress the bear, the more likely you were to think about it.

That's the nature of the thinking mind. It's pretty much always active. It's chattering away while you're waiting in line, when you're trying to solve a difficult task at work, when you "tune out" of conversations with people, or when you're trying to go to sleep.

If your thinking mind starts obsessing over your assignment at work, your observing mind can't stop it. The same applies to emotions. And that's where a lot of our suffering comes from. Not from negative emotions themselves, but from our tendency to helplessly get sucked into them.

Don't Try to Change, Just Observe

Here's the key takeaway in this chapter: most of our negative psychological and emotional experiences happen because we can't tell the difference between our thinking mind and our observing mind.

Most people want to get rid of negative thoughts and feelings. They don't want to feel stress, loneliness, anger, jealousy, and anxiety. And that makes sense. But the thing is, you can't control your thoughts and emotions. Why? Because they belong to your thinking mind. Thoughts and feelings have popped up throughout your life, and they will continue to do so for as long as you live.

What you *can* do, however, is change the way you *relate* to those thoughts and feelings. You can learn not to get sucked into them when they arise. And the way to do that is to pay mindful attention through the observing mind, without getting caught up in the drama of the thinking mind.

The Power of Mindfulness

Jon Kabat-Zinn is a scientist and meditation teacher known for bringing mindfulness into mainstream Western medicine and society. In his book *Full Catastrophe Living*, he defines mindfulness as "paying attention in a particular way: on purpose, in the present moment, and non-judgmentally."

Mindfulness is extremely helpful because it increases your metacognition—your ability to think about your thinking. And the better able you are to do that, the more you can stay with your observing mind instead of getting sucked into the thoughts and feelings of your thinking mind.

Practicing mindfulness means you pay attention to what's going on in your mind and body without judging or getting caught up in it. As you keep practicing, that way of relating to your thoughts and feelings will start spilling over into the rest of your life. Over time, you'll develop a more empowering way to deal with what's going on inside you.

Mindfulness Changes Your Brain

Now, even if you think this concept of the observing and thinking minds sounds a bit hokey, the benefits of mindfulness are rooted in modern science.

Brain imaging studies show that an eight-week course in mindfulness-based stress reduction can be enough to shrink the part of the brain known as the amygdala. That's a primal region of the brain associated with fear and emotion and involved in the body's stress response. Meanwhile, the prefrontal cortex—associated with higher-order brain functions such as awareness, concentration, and decision making—becomes thicker.

Similar to the way physical exercise creates changes in your muscles, mindfulness training creates changes in your brain. And those changes promote a huge number of benefits, including decreased stress, better sleep, happier relationships, less anxiety, and sharper concentration.

And those are just a few examples. The research on mindfulness has exploded lately. More than two thousand scientific articles on the subject have been published at the time of this writing. And with all the amazing benefits being uncovered, it's no surprise many health experts think mindfulness will be the next public health revolution.

Mindfulness and Self-Discipline

Now, besides optimizing your health and well-being, I've found that mindfulness is also a tremendous self-discipline booster.

I used to take my thoughts and feelings very seriously. Whenever one of them showed up, I'd immediately identify with it and adapt to it.

So, if a thought told me that my writing sucks, I'd throw my draft in the trash and do something else. And if I felt restless or bored, I'd immediately look for something else to do.

These days, I know that my thoughts and feelings aren't the "truth." They're simply the result of my thinking mind. And that understanding, combined with consistent mindfulness practice, makes it possible for me to choose a better response.

Instead of getting sucked into my feelings and thoughts, I simply watch them through my observing mind. I let the drama of my thinking mind unfold. I listen to the self-criticism. I feel the self-doubt. Then I do the work anyway. And the more I do that, the less power my thinking mind has over me. The thoughts or feelings that show up rarely control me. Almost always, I'll be able to take action anyway.

That's how I stay self-disciplined. It's how I do the things I don't want to do. And hopefully, I've convinced you to practice mindfulness as well. If so, the first thing you need to do is establish a regular meditation practice. Let's have a look at how to do that next.

How to Meditate

There are a lot of ways to meditate. But our concern is not to find the perfect form of meditation. What's much more important is to create a daily habit of meditation. And to do that, our practice needs to be as simple as possible:

- **Start small.** If you haven't meditated much in the past, or if you've had trouble sticking to the practice, make it ridiculously easy. Commit to just one minute every day. Establish the behavior first. When the practice has become a habit, you can start adding more time to it.

- **Pick a trigger.** Create an if-then plan for your meditation practice. For example, "If I've eaten breakfast, then I will meditate for one minute."

- **Find a quiet place.** Make sure you do your meditation somewhere you can have a couple minutes of undisturbed peace. Early mornings or late evenings are usually good times.

- **Sit comfortably.** You can sit on the floor, on a pillow, in a chair, or on the couch. As long as you're comfortable, you're ready to go.

- **Meditate.** Look at the ground in front of you with a soft gaze or keep your eyes closed. As you breathe in and out, follow your breath all the way from your nostrils to your stomach and back. Sit with your back straight but not tense. If it helps, count: one (inhale), two (exhale), three (inhale), four (exhale). Start over when you get to ten.

And that's it! If you have a lot of intrusive thoughts stealing your attention away from your breath, know that it's perfectly normal. Remember—the practice is not about emptying your head from thoughts but rather changing your relationship to them.

So, all you need to do is gently and nonjudgmentally bring your attention back to the breath every time your mind wanders. If you have to bring it back a hundred times, that's what you do. Every time you bring your attention back to the breath, you are essentially doing one exercise repetition in your mental gym.

Now, while meditation is great practice to learn mindfulness, it's only a small part of your practice. Ideally, you'll want to bring present awareness to everything you do.

Everyday Mindfulness

You can practice mindfulness in everything you do. But, when you're just starting out, it can be helpful to deliberately choose the habits you want to be mindful of every day. For example, you may choose to be mindful of these daily routines:

- **Waking up.** Connect to your breathing as your body is waking up. Before you get up, pay attention to the sights and sounds inside and outside the room.

- **Brushing your teeth.** Try fully concentrating on the action of brushing. Feel each stroke on each tooth, of the toothbrush going from one side of your mouth to the other.

- **Eating breakfast.** Remove all distractions, such as your phone, TV, and newspaper. Instead, pay full attention to each bite of your food.

- **Doing the dishes.** Pay full attention to your washing. Feel the sensations of the warm water on your hands and see the formation of the suds.

- **Walking.** Walk slowly while paying attention to your breath and your surroundings. Be aware of the sounds, the light, and the texture of objects.

As you may suspect by now, I highly recommend a gradual approach. I suggest you start with one habit and then add new ones as you go.

HABIT #4: A QUICK SUMMARY

- According to Zen teachers, you have two minds: the thinking mind and the observing mind.

- You can't control your thinking mind. You can only control your observing mind.

- Most of our negative psychological and emotional experiences happen because we can't tell the difference between our thinking mind and our observing mind.

- Mindfulness is, according to Jon Kabat-Zinn, "paying attention in a particular way: on purpose, in the present moment, and non-judgmentally."

- By applying mindfulness, you can stay with your observing mind instead of getting sucked into your thinking mind. That allows you to stay self-disciplined, moment to moment.

Action Steps

Set Up a Meditation Practice

- ✔ Start small.
- ✔ Pick a trigger.
- ✔ Find a quiet place.
- ✔ Sit comfortably.
- ✔ Meditate.

Choose a Habit for Everyday Mindfulness

✔ Do one of your daily habits in full, present awareness.

Gradually Increase Your Efforts

✔ Once your meditation practice is habitual, incrementally increase the time you spend meditating.

✔ Once you are doing your everyday mindfulness habit consistently, gradually add more of them.

PART 3: SELF-DISCIPLINE STRATEGIES

Show Up and Get to Work

Painter Chuck Close claims he's never had a "painter's block" in his whole life. In an interview for *Inside the Painter's Studio*, he said:

> Inspiration is for amateurs—the rest of us just show up and get to work. And the belief that things will grow out of the activity itself and that you will—through work—bump into other possibilities and kick open other doors that you would never have dreamt of if you were just sitting around looking for a great "art idea." And the belief that process, in a sense, is liberating and that you don't have to reinvent the wheel every day. Today, you know what you'll do, you could be doing what you were doing yesterday, and tomorrow you are gonna do what you did today, and at least for a certain period of time you can just work. If you hang in there, you will get somewhere.

Forget About Motivation

Over the years, a lot of readers have asked me for advice on how to get more motivated. And that makes sense. No matter what you're trying to get done, it's a lot easier when you have that nice feeling of motivation fueling your efforts.

But please note that's exactly what motivation is. It's a *feeling*. And the thing about feelings is that they fluctuate. No one is motivated all the time. So, when you rely on that feeling to take action, you're essentially leaving your most desired outcomes up to chance. Not a good plan.

So, what should you do instead?

Just Show Up and Get to Work

The "just show up and get to work" motto is a great creed to live by in all areas of life. No matter what you want to accomplish, you won't get there by "getting motivated," but by showing up and doing the work every single day.

I know that from my own experience, because when I was relying on motivation and inspiration to write, I'd publish articles very infrequently. But ever since I committed to writing a certain number of hours every day—no matter what—I've published hundreds of articles and two books. Very rarely do I feel inspired or motivated when I sit down to write. But that doesn't matter because I've trained myself to do it anyway.

And no matter what you're trying to achieve, you can train yourself to do it too. All you need to do is put a system in place that makes it second nature for you to show up and do the work.

Create Your Self-Discipline System

Now that we've covered the fundamentals (sleep, nutrition, movement, and mindfulness), it's time to start developing your self-discipline system.

Your system is what's going to make sure you show up and get to work, every single day, whether you feel like it or not.

In the chapters ahead, we'll cover fifteen incredibly powerful self-discipline strategies. I suggest you start by implementing the ones you think will give you the greatest immediate benefits.

And remember, this isn't another chore you have to do—it's an exciting game you get to play with yourself. So, have fun with it!

Run little experiments and tweak the strategies until they work for you. When they are solidly in place, come back and try some new ones, and so on. You can find all the strategies in *The Self-Discipline Blueprint Workbook*.

Inspiration is for amateurs, so let's just show up and get to work!

STRATEGY #1

DEVELOP A GROWTH MINDSET

Some birds and animals cache their food and dig it up later, which means they have to memorize their hiding places.

When researchers studied the brains of these animals, they found something interesting. The part of the brain known as the hippocampus, which plays important roles in memory and spatial navigation, was much larger in these species compared to animals who don't hide their food.

These findings gave neuroscientist Eleanor Maguire the idea to study taxi drivers in London. To earn their licenses, these drivers had spent 3–4 years in training, driving around the city on mopeds and memorizing a labyrinth of twenty-five thousand streets within a ten-kilometer radius of Charing Cross train station, as well as thousands of tourist attractions and hot spots.

Maguire's hypothesis was that, similar to animals who hide their food, London taxi drivers had larger-than-average hippocampi.

The Ever-Changing Brain

To find out if her hypothesis was correct, Maguire and her colleagues analyzed a group of these taxi drivers and compared them to a group of people who did not drive taxis.

The participants' brains were scanned using structural MRI, and the cabbies' brains indeed differed quite a bit from the other participants'. Just like food-hiding animals, the drivers had larger hippocampi. And the volume of that brain region was correlated with the time spent as a taxi driver. The more experience driving a taxi, the larger the hippocampus.

Findings like these are important because, until the 1960s, researchers believed that changes in the brain were possible only during infancy and childhood. It was believed that by early adulthood, the brain's physical structure was permanent.

It's modern research like Eleanor Maguire's that has proven that idea wrong. The brain is "plastic," meaning it creates new neural pathways and alters existing ones all the time. As long as you're alive, your brain is developing.

Fixed versus Growth Mindset

Now, even though researchers know that the brain never stops developing, there's still widespread beliefs that certain qualities are "set in stone." And if you have those beliefs, you'll perform much worse than people who don't have them.

Psychologist Carol Dweck refers to this idea as mindset in her book of the same name. It's a straightforward yet incredibly powerful concept. There are two types of mindsets:

1) **The fixed mindset.** The person believes that his or her basic qualities (like intelligence or talent) are fixed traits.

2) **The growth mindset.** The person believes his or her basic qualities can be developed through dedication and hard work.

The problem with having a fixed mindset is that it makes you feel like you have to prove yourself over and over. After all, if you only have a certain amount of intelligence or talent, it makes sense that you'll want to show you have a lot of it.

119

That desire to look smart makes you avoid challenges, give up easily, ignore useful negative feedback, and feel threatened by the success of others. Since your basic qualities are fixed, you'll see the effort as fruitless and, as a result, you're likely to plateau early and achieve less than your full potential.

A growth mindset, on the other hand, removes the need to prove yourself all the time. When you believe you can overcome your deficiencies, there's no point in hiding them. That would be a waste of time. Instead, you'll have a desire to learn and grow that makes you embrace challenges, persist in the face of setbacks, learn from criticism, and find lessons in the success of others. Since your basic qualities can be developed, you'll see the effort as a path to mastery and, as a result, you'll continually take action to achieve your goals.

It's All in Your Head

Developing a growth mindset is the first strategy in this book for a reason; it's a prerequisite for all the other strategies. If you don't believe you can grow through dedication and hard work, it doesn't matter how many other strategies you learn, because you won't put them to use.

That's why developing a growth mindset is crucial to your success and why I ask you to consider the following:

- Your brain consists of about 100 billion neurons that in turn have up to 50,000 connections to other cells.

- The number of possible connections between these neurons exceeds the number of atoms in the entire universe.

- And, as we've seen in the London taxi drivers, the neural pathways in your brain are constantly adapting to your experience.

You have the most advanced machinery on earth right between your ears, and it's waiting for you to put it into action. It's not your brain, intelligence, or talent that determines your limitations—it's your beliefs about them that do. So, let's get to work on changing those beliefs.

How to Develop a Growth Mindset

Here are Carol Dweck's steps to change from a fixed mindset to growth mindset:

1. Be mindful of your fixed mindset "voice"

As you approach a challenge, all kinds of negative thoughts are likely to pop into your head. Pay attention to what shows up and to what the fixed mindset voice is telling you. Is it saying you can't do it? That you lack talent? Or maybe that you should avoid doing it to stay safe? (Mindfulness practice will help you master this step.)

2. Recognize that you have a choice

How you interpret the thoughts that pop into your mind is completely up to you. You can choose to believe that your talents or abilities are fixed. Or you can decide to ramp up your strategies and effort, stretch yourself, and expand your abilities.

3. Talk back with a growth mindset "voice"

In this step, you'll use a technique that psychologists call cognitive reframing. Your goal is to dispute unhelpful thoughts and replace them with more empowering ones. Here are some examples of what your inner dialogue might sound like, according to Dweck:

> Fixed mindset: "Are you sure you can do it? Maybe you don't have the talent."

> Growth mindset: "I'm not sure I can right now, but I can learn to with time and effort."

> Fixed mindset: "What if you fail? You'll be a failure."

> Growth mindset: "Failing is part of becoming successful."

> Fixed mindset: "If you don't try, you can protect yourself and keep your dignity."

> Growth mindset: "If I don't try, I'll automatically fail. Where's the dignity in that?"

4. Take action

By consistently questioning your fixed mindset voice, poking holes in your limiting beliefs, and choosing more empowering thoughts, you'll find that you are in charge. You get to choose what to do with your thoughts. If they aren't serving you, refute them and take action anyway.

STRATEGY #1: A QUICK SUMMARY

- The brain is "plastic," meaning that it creates new neural pathways and alters existing ones throughout your life.

- People with a fixed mindset believe that their basic qualities (like intelligence or talent) are fixed traits. That creates a desire to look smart.

- People with a growth mindset believe that their basic qualities can be developed through dedication and hard work. That creates a desire to learn and grow.

- Your brain is the most advanced piece of machinery on earth.

- It's not your brain, intelligence, or talent that determines your limitations—it's your beliefs about them that do.

- To realize your potential, you need to develop a growth mindset.

Action Steps

Change from a Fixed Mindset to a Growth Mindset

✔ Be mindful of your fixed mindset "voice."

✔ Recognize that you have a choice.

✔ Talk back with a growth mindset "voice."

✔ Take action.

STRATEGY #2
FIND YOUR MISSION

There's an ancient Greek parable that states: "The fox knows many things, but the hedgehog knows one big thing." In the story, the fox tries every strategy it can think of to catch the hedgehog. It tries sneaking, pouncing, racing, and playing dead.

And yet, every single time, it walks away defeated, with its nose full of spines. The hedgehog always wins because it knows how to do one thing perfectly: defend itself.

In 1953, philosopher Isaiah Berlin took the parable and applied it to the world around him in an essay called *The Hedgehog and the Fox*. He divided people into two groups: foxes and hedgehogs.

Berlin argued that foxes are sleek and shrewd animals who pursue many interests and goals at the same time. Because of that, their thinking is unfocused and scattered, and that limits what they can achieve in the long run.

Hedgehogs, however, are slow and steady in their approach. People often overlook them because they are so quiet and unassuming. But, unlike foxes, they can simplify the world and focus their efforts on one thing. And that helps them succeed against all the odds.

In 2001, leadership expert Jim Collins developed this idea further in his influential book *Good to Great*. According to Collins, organizations are much more likely to succeed if they, like the hedgehog, focus on one thing and do it well.

The Hedgehog Concept

Collins argues that the best companies in every industry stand at the intersection of three critical assessments:

1) What are we deeply passionate about?
2) What can we be the best in the world at?
3) What drives our economic engine?

When an organization has uncovered its Hedgehog Concept, its leaders can devote all their energy and resources to pursuing the one thing it does best. According to Collins, it's that kind of focus that makes for an organization that survives and thrives.

And here's the thing—the Hedgehog Concept is just as useful to you personally as it is for organizations. It's a great model for figuring out your unique mission in life.

In the questions that follow, you'll notice that I've toned down the assessments a bit. That's because I've found wording like "deeply passionate," "best in the world," and "economic engine" to be a bit overwhelming. To avoid getting stuck, we'll start with the following three simple questions instead:

1) What do you like to do?
2) What are you good at?
3) What can you get paid for?

You can find your one thing—your Hedgehog Concept—where these three areas overlap.

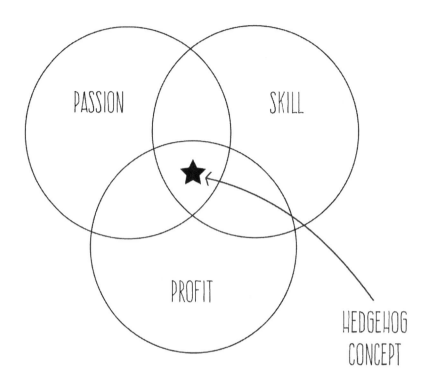

Now, let's drill a little deeper into each of these areas.

1. What You Like to Do

If you can think of things you're deeply passionate about, that's great. But don't get discouraged if you can't. A mere interest can be enough because it can blossom into a passion if you spend a lot of time doing it. To figure out what belongs in this circle, you can ask yourself the following questions:

- What did I spend time doing as a kid?

- What activities absorb me so much that I forget to eat and sleep?

- If money weren't an issue, what would I spend my time doing?

2. What You Are Good At

The next circle is about your unique strengths and skills. These can be surprisingly difficult to pinpoint accurately. That's because they usually come so naturally to us that we don't think of them as strengths or skills. With that in mind, here are some helpful exercises:

- Take a personality test. For example, the Myers-Briggs or the Big Five.

- Take a character strengths test. For example, the VIA Survey.

- Email the people closest to you. Ask them what they consider to be your best strengths and skills and why.

- Ask yourself what people tend to ask you for advice about.

3. What You Can Get Paid For

Finally, you need to combine what you enjoy doing and what you're good at with the needs of the world. You can do that by asking yourself questions like:

- How can my unique interests and strengths be used in the marketplace?

- What jobs match my interests and strengths the best?

- What problems can I solve that people are willing to pay for?

Make Sure That All Three Areas Overlap

Note that having only two of the areas overlapping is a problem:

- If you combine interests and skills, but there's no demand, what you have is most likely a hobby.

- If you combine interests and demand but have no matching skills or strengths, you'll probably struggle to get really good and stand out.

- If you combine skills and demand but have no interest, you'll probably end up with a job you don't like and risk getting burned-out.

The beauty of the Hedgehog Concept is that it uncovers your unique mission in life. Once you've nailed it down, you can spend all your time on one thing. And that thing fits perfectly with your interests and strengths.

So, what the Hedgehog Concept essentially does is set up a game where you're the favorite to win. Again and again and again. And, as we'll learn later in this book, a steady stream of consistent wins creates a strong level of self-discipline.

STRATEGY #2: A QUICK SUMMARY

- "The fox knows many things, but the hedgehog knows one big thing."
- You'll be much more likely to succeed if, like the hedgehog, you focus your energy and resources on one thing.
- The Hedgehog Concept is the overlap between your interests, skills, and the needs of the world.
- By uncovering your unique mission, you set up a game where you're the favorite to win.

Action Steps

Write Down What You Like to Do:

- ✔ What did I spend time doing as a kid?
- ✔ What activities absorb me so much that I forget to eat and sleep?

✔ If money weren't an issue, what would I spend my time doing?

Find Out What You're Good At:

✔ Take a personality test. For example, the Myers-Briggs or the Big Five.

✔ Take a character strengths test. For example, the VIA Survey.

✔ Email the people closest to you. Ask them what they consider to be your best strengths and skills and why.

✔ Ask yourself what people tend to ask you for advice about.

Research What You Can Get Paid For:

✔ How can my unique interests and strengths be used in the marketplace?

✔ What jobs match my interests and strengths the best?

✔ What problems can I solve that people are willing to pay for?

Find your Hedgehog

✔ Notice what lies at the intersection of your interests, skills, and what the world needs. That is your Hedgehog Concept.

STRATEGY #3

KNOW YOUR WHY

Think of how you spent your day today. How did you spend your time? How about the week? The month? The year? Give it some serious thought and then answer this simple question: How much of it truly matters?

Are you spending your time in a way that matters, both to yourself and others? Do you care deeply about what you do? Is it making the world a better place? Are you better as a result?

In his book *Start with Why,* Simon Sinek explains that most people know *what* they do, some even know *how* they do it, but very few know *why* they do what they do.

That's a big problem because it's the *why* part that brings inspiration to everything you do. Your why is the underlying purpose, belief, or cause that drives your actions.

"People Don't Buy What You Do. They Buy *Why* You Do It."

According to Sinek, what separates great companies like Apple from everyone else is that they start with their why. If they presented themselves like most businesses do, their marketing message would look something like this:

"We make great computers. They are beautifully designed, simple to use and user-friendly. Want to buy one?"

Not terribly exciting, is it? And that's not how Apple communicates. Rather, it goes something like this:

"In everything we do, we believe in challenging the status quo. We believe in thinking differently. The way we challenge the status quo is by making our products beautifully designed, simple to use and user-friendly. And we happen to make great computers. Want to buy one?"

A lot more appealing, isn't it? And that's because their message starts with their why, a belief that has nothing to do with what they do. As Sinek says, *"What they do—the products that they make, from computers to small electronics—no longer serves as the reason to buy; they act as the tangible proof of their cause."*

What Do You Do?

How often do you ask people what they do? How often do you tell others what you do? Wouldn't it be much more interesting if, instead, we asked each other *why* we do what we do?

Because let's face it: Very few people care *what* you do. And very few are genuinely interested in *how* you do it. But what they do care about is *why* you do it. So, once you have a clear understanding of your why, you can create a much more powerful connection with others. You can give them a belief to adopt.

And then, your what and how can become great ways to support your why.

You Buy Why You Do It

At this point, you might be wondering what all of this has to do with self-discipline. Well, as it turns out, starting with why isn't just a great way to get others excited about what you do. It's also a crucial piece to put in place to get *yourself* fired up about what you do. Just like you have to persuade others with a compelling why, you have to do the same thing with yourself.

You don't buy what you do; *you* buy why you do it.

Lay Bricks or Build the House of God

In her book *Grit: The Power of Passion and Perseverance*, psychologist Angela Duckworth shares this story:

> Three bricklayers are asked: "What are you doing?"
>
> The first says, "I am laying bricks."
>
> The second says, "I am building a church."
>
> And the third says, "I am building the house of God."
>
> The first bricklayer has a job. The second has a career. The third has a calling.

The difference between a job, a career, and a calling lies in how you perceive the work. You can be doing the same tasks as the person next to you and yet have a vastly different experience.

That is why having a compelling why is so important. It helps you align your daily actions to a bigger purpose. And that, in turn, makes you much more likely to show up and do the work every single day.

The Golden Circle

To find your why, Simon Sinek provides a model called the Golden Circle:

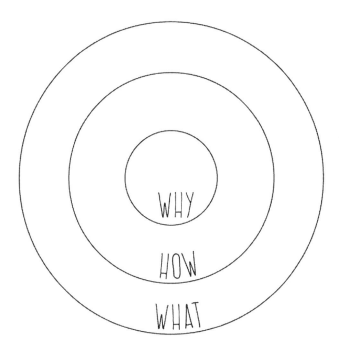

- The what is your job title, function, the products you sell, or the services you offer.

- The how is the actions you take that set you apart from others.

- The why is the purpose, cause, or belief that inspires you.

To give you an example, here's my Golden Circle:

- My what: I'm a mental trainer and writer.

- My how: I write about big ideas and research-backed strategies to help people realize their potential.

- My why: I want to change the world, one person at a time.

Having a meaningful, other-centered purpose like this makes a huge difference in my day-to-day work.

Being a writer isn't all that exciting. But being on a mission to change the world sure is.

Find Your Why

No matter what your current circumstances are, you can find a compelling why.

If you're a student struggling to stay disciplined in school, think about how you can be of service to the world once you graduate.

If you're in a job you don't like, think about how the work you do makes the lives of others easier.

If you're putting yourself through a demanding workout, think about how your improved health and increased energy will benefit the people around you.

Connect what you do to a bigger purpose, and you'll be much more likely to do what you don't want to do.

Remember—you can lay bricks, build a church, or build the house of God. The choice is yours.

STRATEGY #3: A QUICK SUMMARY

- Most people know *what* they do, some even know *how* they do it, but very few know *why* they do what they do.
- "People don't buy *what* you do. They buy *why* you do it."
- *You* don't buy what you do; *you* buy why you do it.
- The Golden Circle consists of your what, your how, and your why.

Action Steps

Write Down Your Golden Circle

✔ Your what—your job title, function, the products you sell, or the services you offer.

✔ Your how—the actions you take that set you apart from others.

✔ Your why—the purpose, cause, or belief that inspires you.

STRATEGY #4

DEFINE YOUR CIRCLE OF COMPETENCE

Warren Buffett is considered one of the most successful investors in the world and consistently ranks among the wealthiest people in the world. In his 1996 shareholder letter, he wrote:

> What an investor needs, is the ability to correctly evaluate selected businesses. Note that word "selected": You don't have to be an expert on every company, or even many. You only have to be able to evaluate companies within your circle of competence. The size of that circle is not very important; knowing its boundaries, however, is vital.

The Circle of Competence

Each of us has built up useful knowledge on certain areas throughout our lives. Some things are understood by most people, while others require a lot more specialty to evaluate.

For example, most of us have a basic understanding of the economics of a restaurant. You buy or rent a place, spend money furnishing it, and then hire employees to cook, seat, serve, and clean. From there, it's a matter of setting the appropriate prices and generating enough traffic to make a profit on the food and drinks you serve. The cuisine, atmosphere, and pricing will vary by restaurant, but they all follow the same economic formula.

That basic knowledge, along with some understanding of accounting and a little bit of study, is enough to evaluate and invest in restaurants. It's not too complicated.

However, most of us don't have the same understanding of the economic formula of a biotech drug company. And, according to Buffett, that's perfectly fine. Being a successful investor doesn't require you to understand every business you come across. It's far more important to understand what you do know—your circle of competence—and then stick to those areas.

Leverage Your Aptitudes

Warren Buffett's right-hand man, Charlie Munger, applies the circle of competence to life in general:

> You have to figure out what your own aptitudes are. If you play games where other people have the aptitudes and you don't, you're going to lose. And that's as close to certain as any prediction that you can make. You have to figure out where you've got an edge. And you've got to play within your own circle of competence.

Just like the Hedgehog Concept, a clearly defined circle of competence ensures you play a game where you're the favorite to win. The better able you are to stick to your circle of competence, the more you'll succeed. And that, in turn, creates an upward spiral where you'll consistently improve and increase your chances of winning even more.

A Personal Example

To give you a concrete example, I'll share my circle of competence. It contains three major areas:

1) **Writing.** This is the number one keystone habit of my business. So, before I do anything else each day, I write for at least two

hours. That allows me to publish new material and develop my craft consistently.

2) **Learning.** To be a good writer, I need a lot of good ideas to write about. So, I spend time every day educating myself on things my readers want to learn about—behavior change, motivation, mental toughness, and so on.

3) **Marketing.** To be a successful writer, I need to reach and serve as many people as possible. To do that, I have to be good at promoting my work. So, I also spend a lot of time learning about stuff like online marketing, persuasion, consumer psychology, and so on.

Knowing my circle of competence allows me to focus my efforts much more efficiently. Each day that I learn something, write something, and promote what I wrote is a day well spent. I stuck to, and strengthened, my circle of competence. And each day I do that I consider a win.

Individual Fundamentals

In part 2 of this book, we covered the fundamental habits of self-discipline: sleep, nutrition, movement, and mindfulness. These are *universal* fundamentals that everyone needs to take care of their health and perform at their very best.

This chapter is about your *individual* fundamentals. Your circle of competence tells you what you should focus on to make the most out of your time and efforts.

Look back at your mission (strategy #2) and your why (strategy #3), and ask yourself: What are the three most important areas I need to focus on? Where should I spend my time and effort to align with my why and succeed at my mission? What particular habits do I need to create to stay within, and strengthen, my circle of competence every day?

Once you've uncovered your individual fundamentals, you can move forward with a great sense of clarity, direction, and confidence in your daily actions.

STRATEGY #4: A QUICK SUMMARY

- Your circle of competence is useful knowledge on certain areas that you've acquired throughout your life.

- The size of your circle is not very important, but knowing its boundaries is vital.

- Having a clearly defined circle of competence ensures you play a game where you're the favorite to win.

- Your circle of competence contains your individual fundamentals—the actions you should focus on to make the most out of your time and efforts.

Action Steps

Write Down Your Circle of Competence

- ✔ What are the three most important areas I need to focus on?

- ✔ Where should I spend my time and effort to align with my why and succeed at my mission?

- ✔ What habits do I need to create to strengthen my circle of competence every day?

Make Room For Your Fundamentals

- ✔ Schedule time for each of your individual fundamental habits in your calendar.

STRATEGY #5
MEASURE YOUR PROGRESS

Are you familiar with comedian Jerry Seinfeld's "Don't break the chain" strategy? If not, I'll share the story about it briefly.

A young comedian was just starting out on the comedy circuit and, at one point, he found himself in the same club where Jerry Seinfeld was performing.

In an interview with Lifehacker, the up-and-coming comedian shared what happened as he approached Seinfeld backstage and asked if he had any advice for a young comic.

Seinfeld's Productivity Secret

Here's how the young comedian described his interaction with Seinfeld:

> He said the way to be a better comic was to create better jokes and the way to create better jokes was to write every day.

> He told me to get a big wall calendar that has a whole year on one page and hang it on a prominent wall. The next step was to get a big red magic marker.

> He said for each day that I do my task of writing, I get to put a big red X on that day. "After a few days you'll have a chain. Just keep at it and the chain will grow longer every day. You'll like seeing that chain, especially when you get a few weeks under your belt. Your only job is to not break the chain."

An Unexpected Twist

Now, if you've already heard about Seinfeld's "Don't break the chain" strategy, that's no surprise.

It's been written about time and time again in articles, magazines, and books. I even included it in my first book, *The Habit Blueprint*.

But here's the unexpected twist: Jerry Seinfeld never came up with, or even used, the strategy himself. That's right. In a 2014 "Ask Me Anything" session on Reddit, he wrote, "This is hilarious to me, that somehow I am getting credit for making an X on a calendar with the Seinfeld productivity program. It's the dumbest non-idea that was not mine, but somehow I'm getting credit for it."

What You Measure Gets Improved

I find it kind of funny how Seinfeld's productivity "secret" turned out to have nothing to do with Jerry Seinfeld. But I don't agree that it's a "dumb non-idea."

What gets measured gets improved. The simple act of paying attention to something will help you make connections you never did before. You'll spot recurring obstacles and come up with solutions.

And, no matter who invented it, the "Don't break the chain" concept provides a simple and effective way to start measuring what you do.

So, to make sure that you're consistently working on and strengthening your fundamentals, I warmly encourage you to start building your own chain. Let's have a close look at how to do that.

1. Get a Calendar and Marker

There are many different kinds of calendars you can use to track your progress. I use a monthly calendar that shows the dates on the far left and has several empty grids on the right. That way, I can check off all my daily habits in one space. It looks something like this:

HABITS					
1					
2					
3					
4					
5					
6					
7					
8					
9					
10					
11					
12					
13					
14					
15					
16					
17					
18					
19					
20					
21					
22					
23					
24					
25					
26					
27					
28					
29					
30					
31					

It doesn't matter which kind you use, though. The important thing is you find a calendar and marker you like. You'll want the act of writing down big X's to become a reward you look forward to every day.

2. Set Your Daily Minimums

Next, you need to decide the minimum amount of effort you're required to accomplish every day to earn the X's on your calendar. I recommend starting with small daily targets that allow you to experience easy wins. Create one for all of your fundamental keystone habits. For example:

- **Sleep.** Do a one-minute breathing exercise to relax.
- **Nutrition.** Eat a piece of fruit in the afternoon.
- **Movement.** Take the stairs.
- **Mindfulness.** Meditate for two minutes.

Then create one for each area in your circle of competence. For example:

- **Writing.** Write two hundred words.
- **Learning.** Read two pages in a book.
- **Marketing.** Send a helpful email to a reader.

Each day that you accomplish your minimum daily effort, put a big X on your calendar. Great job!

3. Establish Your Rules

It's unrealistic to expect yourself to stick with all your habits every day for an entire year. Sometimes, you'll want to take a break and sometimes you'll get sick.

On these occasions, I recommend putting down other letters on your calendar. For example, if you are on vacation, you can write a V on that day. If you're sick, you can put down an S.

Set very unambiguous rules for special occasions when you'll permit yourself to skip your habits. That way, you'll be able to keep your chain going when you have legit reasons to miss a certain number of days.

4. Get Started

Once you have your calendar, minimums, and rules in place, I encourage you to get started right away.

Not only will your chains provide a great incentive to stick to your habits, they will also provide valuable data you can use to become increasingly more efficient.

Continually ask yourself why your chains are developing the way they are. If one is particularly successful, why is that? If one tends to break often, why is that?

That way, you'll set yourself up for continual improvement and become increasingly efficient in everything that you do.

STRATEGY #5: A QUICK SUMMARY

- What gets measured gets improved.
- An effective way of measuring and improving is using Jerry Seinfeld's "Don't break the chain" strategy . . .
- that turned out having nothing to do with Jerry Seinfeld.

Actions Steps

Start Measuring Your Fundamental Keystone Habits

✔ Get a calendar and marker.

✔ Set your daily minimums.

✔ Establish your rules.

✔ Get started!

STRATEGY #6

CREATE A WINNER EFFECT

In 1995, legendary boxer Mike Tyson was getting ready to get back into the ring after serving three years in prison.

To prepare him for his WBC title match against the current champion, Frank Bruno, Tyson's promoter, Don King, arranged two preparation fights.

You might think King would want to prepare Tyson by arranging fights against two great boxers. But he did the exact opposite.

King scheduled matches against what's known in boxing circles as tomato cans—fighters that are clearly inferior and easy to beat.

Fighting Tomato Cans

Tyson won his first comeback match against Peter McNeeley on knockout after eighty-nine seconds.

A few months later, he faced his second opponent, Buster Mathis Jr. That fight took a bit longer. It took Tyson until the last minute of the third round to finally defeat his overweight opponent.

At that point, a lot of questions were being asked. Why did King choose to prepare Tyson like that? Why did he arrange fights against two clearly inferior fighters? Wouldn't that risk getting Tyson ridiculed, weakening his self-belief and putting the renewal of his career in jeopardy?

But in the spring of 1996, all the critics were silenced. That's when Tyson knocked out Frank Bruno in the third round of the WBC championship and reclaimed the title as world champion.

And whether he knew it or not, Don King had prepared Tyson perfectly according to a powerful psychological principle.

The Winner Effect

According to neuropsychologist Ian Robertson, success and failure shape us more powerfully than anything else. In his book *The Winner Effect*, he explains that an animal that has won a few fights against weak opponents is much more likely to win future confrontations against stronger contenders. That's true across all species—humans included.

The reason that happens is that success changes the chemistry of the brain. Each time you win, there's an increase of testosterone and dopamine in your body. And those chemicals make you more confident, more aggressive, more focused, and smarter. Your mind and body essentially reshape to give you a biological advantage in the future. And the more you win, the more likely you'll be to win in the future.

The Progress Principle

Now, in case you're wondering, you don't have to engage in actual fistfights to benefit from easy wins. Setting yourself up for success in your daily routine tasks can also be very effective.

Teresa Amabile from the Harvard Business School studies how everyday life inside organizations can influence people and their performance. When she and her associates designed and analyzed nearly twelve thousand diary entries from 238 employees in seven companies, they uncovered what they now call *The Progress Principle*:

> Of all the things that can boost emotions, motivation, and perceptions during a workday, the single most important is making progress in meaningful work. And the more frequently people experience that sense of progress, the more likely they are to be creatively productive in the long run. Whether they are trying to solve a major scientific mystery or simply produce a high-quality product or service, everyday progress—even a small win—can make all the difference in how they feel and perform.

Line Up Your Tomato Cans

No matter what you want to achieve, you'll increase your chances dramatically by allowing yourself to experience success. And the way you make that happen is by lining up, and knocking down, your own set of "tomato cans"—goals that are so easy that you're pretty much guaranteed to win.

In the last chapter, we covered how to set your minimum daily targets. The reason I suggest you make them so small is because that's how you turn them into tomato cans. Let's have a look at the examples one more time:

Universal fundamentals

- **Sleep.** Do a one-minute breathing exercise to relax.
- **Nutrition.** Eat a piece of fruit in the afternoon.
- **Movement.** Take the stairs.
- **Mindfulness.** Meditate for two minutes.

<u>Individual fundamentals</u>

- **Writing.** Write two hundred words.

- **Learning.** Read two pages in a book.

- **Marketing.** Send a helpful email to a reader.

By making your daily goals that easy, you'll ensure that you experience consistent success. That success will create a powerful winner effect. And the winner effect will create the progress and momentum necessary to move you through more challenging goals in the future.

STRATEGY #6: A QUICK SUMMARY

- Success and failure shape us more powerfully than anything else.

- An animal that has won a few fights against weaker opponents is much more likely to win future confrontations against stronger contenders. That's the winner effect.

- The single most important thing to boost emotions, motivation, and perception is to make progress in meaningful work. That's the progress principle.

Action Steps

Review Your Minimum Daily Targets

- ✔ Ask yourself if they truly are tomato cans. In other words, are they so easy that you're pretty much guaranteed to win? If so, great! You can move on to the next chapter. But if not, take the time right now to make them so easy that you're very confident in your ability to get them done every day. And don't worry if you feel like they're so small they won't allow you to make enough progress. We'll address that in strategy #9.

STRATEGY #7

REWARD YOURSELF

Times are few and far between when someone is excited about getting a ticket from the police. Unless you're in the particularly innovative police precinct in Richmond, Canada, that is.

In that area, police officers regularly hand out "positive tickets" to youngsters who are exhibiting positive behaviors like picking up litter or crossing the road safely.

The positive tickets can be exchanged for things like free hamburgers, cinema tickets, or the possibility to see a game with the local hockey team, all of which have been donated by local businesses.

The purpose of handing out positive tickets is to reward young people who make healthy, positive choices in relation to their behavior, decisions, and actions.

The Power of Positive Tickets

There is a well-established, best-practice approach to deal with crime: pass harsher laws, set stronger sentencing, or initiate zero-tolerance initiatives. In other words, we tend to have a strong preference for punishing bad behavior.

But the positive-ticket practice has shown that there are a lot of benefits to be had from also rewarding good behavior.

Before implementing their positive tickets, the district had a recidivism (repeat offender) rate of 65 percent and spiraling rates of youth crime.

After adding positive tickets to their repertoire, recidivism was reduced to 5 percent, and youth crime was cut in half.

Rewards Are Crucial for Success

The justice system reflects human psychology. Just as law enforcement is biased toward punishment rather than reward, so are we as individuals.

Whenever we make a mistake, we immediately punish ourselves for it. We berate ourselves for what we did and feel guilty about it.

But whenever we do something well, we usually don't reward ourselves. Instead, we tell ourselves it wasn't a big deal and that it isn't worth boasting about. And that's a big problem. Not only because we end up experiencing more negative feelings than positive ones but also because it ruins our chances to build confidence, motivation, and momentum.

As we covered in the last chapter, easy wins are crucial parts of the winner effect and the progress principle. To get it going, you have to allow yourself to experience the feeling of success consistently.

B. F. Skinner's Token Economy

What you need to do is to create your personal "positive ticketing" system. You have to find opportunities to reward your good behavior.

Psychologist Neil Fiore has a great strategy for doing that. In his book *The Now Habit*, he writes about how, as a student, he was looking for a way to overcome his procrastination.

While searching for a solution, he found out that B. F. Skinner, the founder of modern behaviorism, used a time clock connected to his chair to "punch in" each time he sat down to work. Whenever he got up from his chair, the clock would stop as if he were "punching out." That way, Skinner could measure his time much like architects and lawyers do when they keep track of the time to charge their clients.

Skinner recorded his times in flow charts, and each time he completed a small segment of work, he awarded himself with a gold star.

The strategy of giving out gold stars or other symbols for rewarding and reinforcing good behavior is known in psychology as a token economy.

Just like the positive tickets, these tokens can later be exchanged for real rewards.

How to Create Your Token Economy

1. Choose tokens to reward yourself with

Tokens could be gold stars, coins, poker chips, or something else you have lying around the house. Each time you successfully reach your minimum daily target, reward yourself with a token. Then start stacking your tokens somewhere you can see them every day. With time, that will create an inspiring visual representation of your progress.

2. Create a list of inspiring rewards

These are the things you get to exchange your tokens for. The key here is to reward yourself with things that keep you moving toward, and not away from, your long-term goals. In other words, don't celebrate a good week of running by eating chocolate cake but rather by getting a new piece of running equipment.

Create a list of rewards that allows you to progressively build the identity of the person you want to become. For the running example, your list could look something like this:

- Water bottle = 5 tokens
- Running socks = 10 tokens
- Pedometer = 50 tokens
- Running shoes = 100 tokens
- Entry to marathon = 500 tokens

That is not a perfect token economy by any means, but I'm sure you get the point. What's important is that you create a list of rewards that give you an increasing sense of accomplishment and competence.

STRATEGY #7: A QUICK SUMMARY

- We're very good at punishing ourselves and very bad at rewarding ourselves.
- That is a big problem because rewarding yourself is crucial to building confidence, motivation, and momentum.
- You need easy wins to take advantage of the winner effect and the progress principle.
- A token economy is an excellent way to reward and reinforce good behavior.

Action Steps

Create a Token Economy

- ✔ Choose the tokens to reward yourself with.
- ✔ Create a list of inspiring rewards.
- ✔ Start rewarding yourself for your good behaviors.

STRATEGY #8

USE COMMITMENT DEVICES

Throughout history, people have used many strategies to commit themselves to what they want and need to get done.

A classic prototypical example is the story of Odysseus. He ordered his men to plug their ears with beeswax and tie his body to the mast of the ship, so he could listen to the songs of the sirens without being lured into jumping overboard.

Another is Spanish conqueror Hernán Cortés's bold move to destroy his ships to remove the possibility of retreat and thereby increase the chances of his men defeating the Mayans.

These stories are great metaphors for everyday life. Just like Odysseus, you have modern sirens trying to seduce you: social media, email, games, apps, movies, and TV series are constantly "calling for you," offering an easier and immediately gratifying alternative to what you're doing.

And just like Cortés, you have your own conquests to make. That could be things like writing an essay for school, finishing a report for work, sticking to an exercise routine, and so on. Those are all personal quests that require you to stay the course and not retreat.

Akrasia

If you're struggling to stick to your goals, you're not alone. It's a problem people have had throughout recorded history. In fact, philosophers all the way back to Plato and Aristotle even created their own word for it. They called it "akrasia," and it encompasses procrastination, lack of self-control, lack of follow-through, and any kind of addictive behavior.

Why do we have this problem? The technical answer is "time inconsistency," and it's nicely illustrated in a study on grocery-buying habits. When buying groceries online for delivery tomorrow, people purchase a lot more ice cream and a lot fewer vegetables than when they're ordering for delivery next week.

In other words, our preferences are inconsistent over time. We want what we know is good for us. Just not right now. And the problem with that, of course, is that we are always in the now.

Commitment Devices

So, how do you overcome akrasia? Well, you use the strategies of Odysseus and Hernán Cortés. If you know sirens will be seducing you later, you tie yourself to the mast. If you have a conquest to make, you destroy the ships behind you.

These days, strategies like these are called commitment devices, and they can come in many forms. Here are a few examples:

- Cutting up your credit cards to avoid mindless spending.
- Leaving your laptop in the office so you can't keep working from home.
- Buying junk food or candy in small packages.
- Getting rid of all alcohol in your house to prevent drinking.
- Buying small plates to avoid overeating.
- Teaming up with a workout partner for accountability.
- Having a portion of your paycheck automatically transferred to your savings account.

- Canceling your TV service to protect your time.

There are also a number of services you can use to bind yourself to your goals. Here are the two most popular ones:

- stickK lets you create and sign a "commitment contract." You set a start and end date, assign a referee to hold you accountable, and add supporters to cheer you on. If you want, you can also put some money on the line and have stickK send it to a charity or organization you don't like if you fail.

- Beeminder combines commitment contracts with self-tracking. Your challenge here is to keep all your data points on a Yellow Brick Road. If you fail to do that, you lose the money you've put at stake.

And if you want to beat akrasia online, there are tons of apps and extensions to help you do that. Check out the following examples:

- News Feed Eradicator for Facebook is a Chrome extension that replaces your Facebook news feed with an inspiring quote.

- Freedom is an app for Mac that allows you to lock yourself away from the Internet so you can become more productive.

- SelfControl is an app for Mac that lets you block your access to sites and email servers for a set amount of time.

- StayFocusd is a Chrome extension that allows you to restrict the amount of time you can spend on time-wasting websites.

- Forest is a clever way to stay off your phone when you should be working. The app lets you plant a digital tree whenever you want to focus. The tree will then grow during the next thirty minutes, but if you leave the app, the tree will die. If you stay committed, you'll plant a forest.

Get Creative!

As you can see, there are tons of ways you can use commitment devices to overcome akrasia. And these are by no means exhaustive lists. Author Maneesh Sethi invented the funniest commitment device I've heard about.

To beat his online procrastination, he hired a "slapper" to smack him in the face whenever he logged on to Facebook. With this commitment device in place, his productivity skyrocket from 38 percent to 98 percent.

Now, if you think hiring someone to hit you is a bit extreme, I certainly agree. But I encourage you to get as creative with this as Sethi did. You are the biggest expert in the world on your own psychology, so you're best qualified to find commitment devices that work for you.

Maybe you need to block social media sites during work hours. Maybe you need to put some money at stake. Maybe you need to put your TV in the garage. What kind of commitment devices you use doesn't matter—as long as they get you the results you're after.

STRATEGY #8: A QUICK SUMMARY

- "Akrasia" is the ancient word for the failure of the will. It encompasses procrastination, lack of self-control, lack of fol-low-through, and any kind of addictive behavior.

- Time inconsistency tells us our preferences are inconsistent over time. We want what we know is good for us—just not right now.

- To overcome akrasia and time inconsistency, you can use commitment devices to change the incentives and "burn your ships" and "tie yourself" to a particular course of action.

Action Steps

Set Up Your Commitment Devices

✔ Go through your list of minimum daily targets. Think about what strategies, services, apps, and extensions you can put in place to avoid akrasia in all of them. Then put them all in place.

STRATEGY #9

MAKE MARGINAL GAINS

In sports science theory, there is a fundamental principle of athletic training known as supercompensation. How's that for a badass word?

The concept of supercompensation refers to "the post-training period during which the trained function/parameter has a higher performance capacity than it did prior to the training period."

The idea is that, since the human body is an adjustable organism, it will not only recover from the exercise—it will adapt to the new strain placed on it and get a little bit stronger than it was before.

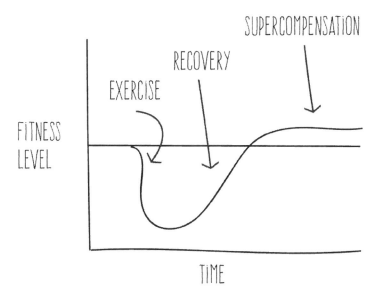

But here's the thing: supercompensation will only occur if you increase your efforts to a level that is higher than what your body is already used to. And that's unfortunately where a lot of people get it wrong. According to sports scientists, the most common mistake people make when exercising is that they do the same workout over and over again.

Lifting the same weights and running the same trail at the same pace will not increase your strength and endurance. That's because, when you exercise that way, there's no new level of strain for your body to adapt to. And because of that, no supercompensation will occur.

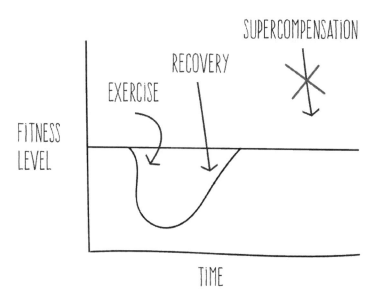

Albert Einstein allegedly said that the definition of insanity is doing the same thing over and over again, but expecting different results.

So, if you want your fitness level to improve, you can't keep doing the exact same workout week in and week out. That would be crazy. Literally. Hey, it was Einstein who said it, not me.

For supercompensation to occur, you need to consistently push yourself to levels you're not used to. Each new workout has to be a little more challenging than the last. You need to lift slightly heavier weights and run a little bit farther or faster than you did before.

The Supercompensation of Habits

The concept of supercompensation isn't helpful just for fitness. It's very handy for every habit in your life. Let's have yet another look at the examples from the previous chapters:

Universal fundamentals

- **Sleep.** Do a one-minute breathing exercise to relax.
- **Nutrition.** Eat a piece of fruit in the afternoon.
- **Movement.** Take the stairs.
- **Mindfulness.** Meditate for two minutes.

Individual fundamentals

- **Writing.** Write two hundred words.
- **Learning.** Read two pages in a book.
- **Marketing.** Send a helpful email to a reader.

As we've already covered, these minimum daily targets are great tomato cans. They help you get started, build momentum, and quickly establish new habits. But once they're in place, it's important that you don't settle for putting in the same amount of effort every day. If you do, your growth will quickly plateau.

Instead, you should consistently look for ways to make marginal gains—consistently raise the bar just a little bit and push yourself to get slightly better at everything you do.

Marginal Gains in Life

There are two ways to make marginal gains in your life. You can either keep adding new small habits or increase the efforts of your already existing ones. Here are some ideas:

Universal fundamentals

- **Sleep.** Make one small improvement in your evening routine every week.

- **Nutrition.** Remove one type of unhealthy food from your diet every week.

- **Movement.** Add a new micro, mini, or macro movement every week.

- **Mindfulness.** Extend your meditation practice by one minute every month.

Individual fundamentals

- **Writing.** Add one hundred words to your daily writing goal every month.

- **Learning.** Add one more page to your daily reading goal every month.

- **Marketing.** Send one additional helpful email to readers every month.

These are just a few examples, of course. Hopefully, they will give you some ideas for how you can create marginal gains in your life. Because that's when supercompensation occurs, and that's how you create remarkable results over time.

Your Weekly Review

To make sure that you are consistently making marginal gains in your habits, you need to follow up on them consistently. And an excellent way to do that is to schedule a weekly review—a recurring block of time you use to review the past week and prepare yourself for the upcoming week. Here's a step-by-step process you can use:

1) **Analyze your progress.** Review the chains in your calendar to see which habits went well and which didn't.

2) **Reward yourself.** Give yourself tokens for every successful completion of your minimum daily targets.

3) **Exchange your tokens.** If you have enough tokens, you can exchange them for real rewards.

4) **Readjust your approach.** If you failed at any of your habits, analyze what went wrong and put strategies in place to improve your performance next week.

5) **Make marginal gains.** If you had a successful seven-day streak in any of your habits, ask yourself how you can slightly increase the effort for next week.

STRATEGY #9: A QUICK SUMMARY

- Supercompensation says that, since the human body is an adjustable organism, it will not only recover from exercise—it will adapt to the new strain placed on it and get a little bit stronger than it was before.

- For supercompensation to occur, you need to increase your efforts to a level that is higher than what your body is already used to.

- You can apply the concept of supercompensation to your life by consistently adding new small habits or increasing the efforts of your already existing ones.

Action Steps

Schedule a Weekly Review

✔ Plan a recurring thirty-minute block of time to walk through the following steps:

1. Analyze your progress.

2. Reward yourself.

3. Exchange your tokens.

4. Readjust your approach.

5. Make marginal gains.

STRATEGY #10

MANAGE YOUR ENERGY

When author Michael Lewis was preparing an article featuring former President Barack Obama, the two of them spent six months in close company.

Lewis got to hang out in the White House, sit up front in the Air Force One, participate in the president's private basketball games, and talk with him whenever he had a moment.

On one occasion, Lewis presented Obama with this scenario: "Assume that in 30 minutes you will stop being president. I will take your place. Prepare me. Teach me how to be president."

Obama answered: "You'll see I wear only gray or blue suits. I'm trying to pare down decisions. I don't want to make decisions about what I'm eating or wearing. Because I have too many other decisions to make. . . . You need to focus your decision-making energy. You need to routinize yourself. You can't be going through the day distracted by trivia."

Decision Fatigue

Whether Obama knew it or not, his ideas are backed by science. Psychologists refer to it as decision fatigue: "the deteriorating quality of decisions made by an individual after a long session of decision making."

The concept was illustrated nicely in a 2011 study in which a group of researchers examined the factors impacting whether judges approve criminals for parole. After reviewing 1,112 judicial rulings over a ten-month period, they found something interesting.

The judges' decisions weren't based just on the things you might expect, such as the type of crime committed or the particular laws that had been broken. There were a lot of other factors that impacted the judges, many of which shouldn't have an effect in the courtroom. Most notable of these was the time of day.

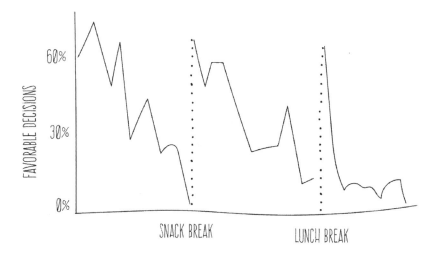

At the beginning of the day, a judge was likely to give the criminal a favorable ruling about 65 percent of the time. Then, as the morning wore on, the judge became drained by making more and more decisions. And as fatigue kept increasing, the likelihood of obtaining a favorable ruling steadily dropped to zero before lunchtime.

After lunch, the judge would come back refreshed, and the probability of a favorable ruling would immediately jump back up to about 65 percent. The same scenario would then play out in the afternoon. The judge got more and more tired, and at the end of the day, the chances of a favorable ruling were down to zero once again. This trend held true for all 1,112 cases, no matter what the crime.

Is this fair? No. But it does make sense. When you're getting tired from making a lot of decisions, it's easier and safer to say no and keep everyone locked up than to try to determine whether someone is trustworthy enough to leave prison.

Manage Your Energy

So, how is all of this important to you? Well, decision fatigue is taking place every day in your life as well. If you've ever come home from a particularly decision-heavy day at school or work, you know what I mean.

You might want to hit the gym and work out, but your brain would much prefer you stay put on the couch. That's decision fatigue, and if you want to develop your self-discipline, you need to employ certain strategies to overcome it. Here's how.

1. Make Fewer Unimportant Decisions

If the first thing you do when you wake up in the morning is ask yourself what to wear, what to eat for breakfast, how to get to work, and so on, you'll start running out of mental energy before even starting your day. So, what you need to do, just like Obama said, is routinize yourself.

If your days are anything like mine, they tend to have a lot of unforeseen events that make them very hard to routinize. But you probably have a little more control over your mornings and evenings. And that's why these are great times to set yourself up for productive days:

- **Use an evening routine to prepare for the next day.** For example, clean up around the house, prepare your lunch for the next day, and write down your most important tasks for tomorrow. Then get your body ready for a good night's sleep.

- **Use a morning routine to set yourself up for a great day.** Run a predetermined set of habits to prepare your body and mind for the day. For example, do a quick workout, meditate, and review your most important tasks. Then get to work.

2. Do the Right Work at the Right Time

I always get my writing done directly after my morning routine. Why? Because I know that's when my energy is highest, and my brain is sharpest. Writing is the most demanding work I do each day, so I make sure to do it when I'm in my peak state.

Only after I've finished my writing for the day do I turn on my phone, open my email, and deal with other tasks related to my business. These things are important, too. But they're not as demanding as my writing. So, I deal with them in the afternoon when my energy is usually a bit lower. The late afternoon is when I typically do my best lifting, so that's when I go to the gym.

To be clear, my schedule didn't always look like that. It took a lot of trial and error to find out how to best manage my energy. But once I did, it made a huge difference in my productivity.

So, I highly recommend you start experimenting with these things as well. Ask yourself when your energy tends to be at its highest and lowest. Then rearrange your daily activities accordingly.

STRATEGY #10: A QUICK SUMMARY

- Decision fatigue is "the deteriorating quality of decisions made by an individual after a long session of decision making."

- To avoid decision fatigue, you need to manage your energy.

- You can manage your energy by making fewer unimportant decisions and by doing the right work at the right time.

Action Steps

Manage Your Daily Energy

- ✔ Create an evening routine to prepare for the next day.

- ✔ Use a morning routine to set yourself up for a great day.

- ✔ Rearrange your schedule to match your energy levels throughout the day.

STRATEGY #11

PROTECT YOUR TIME

In his essay "On the Shortness of Life," the Roman Stoic philosopher Seneca writes that people suffer from a "foolish forgetfulness of our mortality" and reminds us that if we waste our life, nature will not give us any warnings. Instead, life will silently glide away:

> It is not that we have a short time to live, but that we waste a lot of it. Life is long enough, and a sufficiently generous amount has been given to us for the highest achievements if it were all well invested. But when it is wasted in heedless luxury and spent on no good activity, we are forced at last by death's final constraint to realize that it has passed away before we knew it was passing. So it is: we are not given a short life but we make it short, and we are not ill-supplied but wasteful of it. . . . Life is long if you know how to use it.

Protect Your Time

Your time is your most valuable resource. Unlike money, it's a non-renewable. You can always get more money, but you can never get more time.

And still, we tend to be much more careful with our money than we are with our time. If someone tries to take our money, we're usually very protective of it. But if someone tries to take our time, we often don't think twice about giving it away.

If you want to be a highly disciplined person, you can't afford to give away your most precious resource. You have to realize how valuable it is and protect it accordingly.

That's the only way to make meaningful progress on the things that matter to you. And it's the only way to not let your life silently glide away.

Become an Essentialist

In his book *Essentialism*, Greg McKeown writes:

> The way of the Essentialist means living by design, not by default. Instead of making choices reactively, the Essentialist deliberately distinguishes the vital few from the trivial many, eliminates the nonessentials, and then removes obstacles so the essential things have clear, smooth passage.

Once you've determined what's important to you—your mission, your why, and your fundamentals—you need to ruthlessly cut out the distractions that are getting in their way. Instead of trying to get more done in less time, focus on only getting the right things done. Let's have a look at some powerful ways of doing that.

1. Cut Out TV

The average person will spend nine years of their life watching TV. Just imagine how much potential could be unleashed if instead that time was spent developing skills and realizing dreams. Avoid mindless zapping. Instead, proactively decide how much time you're willing to spend watching TV every day. Deliberately and carefully select the shows you actually want to watch. Then turn the TV off.

2. Limit Internet Usage

Proactively restrict the time you spend surfing the web. Limit access to time-sucking websites and block social media sites when you don't need them. There are several useful apps available for doing that. Revisit strategy #8 for some suggestions.

3. Reorganize Your Phone

We check our phones on average 150 times per day. Each time you unlock to see all the apps and red badges signaling what you've missed, you risk getting sucked into nonessentials. So, remove all notifications from your phone. And then delete or move time-wasting apps from your home screen.

4. Reduce Your Email

Decide when you're going to check your email inbox every day. Ideally, this would be late in the day, so you don't risk getting pulled into time-wasters before you've finished your most important work. Remove email notifications from all your devices and relentlessly unsubscribe from newsletters you don't need.

5. Simplify Your Commitments

Question all your obligations. Are they truly as important as you think? Or are they stealing time from what's essential? Experiment with temporarily cutting out or delegating commitments. See if you suffer from it or if you enjoy the extra time. We're usually not as indispensable as we think.

6. Say No

Every time you say yes to something unimportant, you say no to something important. So, be very careful what you say yes to. In the words of Derek Sivers, it's either "HELL YEAH!" or no. Learn to decline politely and quickly get back to what's important. And don't be apologetic about it. Instead, be proud of your ability to protect your time.

STRATEGY #11: A QUICK SUMMARY

- "We are not given a short life, but we make it short, and we are not ill-supplied but wasteful of it. Life is long if you know how to use it."

- Time is more valuable than money. You can always get more money, but you can never get more time.

- To be a highly disciplined person, you need to give your time the protection it deserves.

- Become an essentialist; instead of trying to get more done in less time, focus only on getting the right things done.

Action Steps

Save Your Time for What's Essential

- ✔ Cut out TV.
- ✔ Limit Internet usage.
- ✔ Reorganize your phone.
- ✔ Reduce your email.
- ✔ Simplify your commitments.
- ✔ Say no.

STRATEGY #12

SHAPE YOUR ENVIRONMENT

We often assume that we do what we do because of *who* we are. But the truth is, a lot of what we do is the result of *where* we are.

A fascinating study by researchers Eric Johnson and Daniel Goldstein beautifully illustrate that point. They investigated the answers people gave to the following question.

"Would You Like to Be an Organ Donor?"

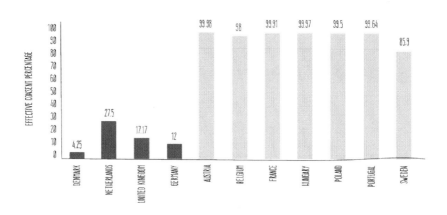

EFFECTIVE CONSENT RATES, BY COUNTRY. EXPLICIT CONSENT (OPT-IN, GOLD) AND PRESUMED CONSENT (OPT-OUT, BLUE)

This graph shows the percentage of people across a number of European countries who are willing to donate their organs after they die.

As you can see, there's a *huge* difference between the countries on the left and the ones on the right. How can that be?

At first glance, you may think some big reason like culture or religion caused these results, but at a closer look, that doesn't hold up.

Denmark and Sweden, the Netherlands and Belgium, Austria and Germany—these are all countries with similar cultures and religious beliefs. Still, their organ donation percentages are wildly different. So, what's going on here?

The Default Effect

It's actually quite simple. What explains the differences between the countries is the design of the form related to the organ donations in each region.

In the countries where the form has an "opt-in" design (i.e., "Check this box if you *want* to donate your organs"), people tend not to check the box.

And in the countries where the form has an "opt-out" design (i.e., "Check this box if you *don't want* to donate your organs"), people *also* tend not to check the box.

No matter which one of these forms people are presented with, an overwhelming majority of them will choose to stay with what they already have.

In psychology, this tendency is called the default effect, and it takes place all the time as we go about our daily business.

What Are Your Default Options?

We rarely pay attention to them, but the default options surrounding us every day have a huge effect on our behavior:

- If we have snacks on the table, we're likely to eat them.

- If we have a remote control on the living room table, we're likely to turn on the TV.

- If we sleep with our phone next to our bed, we're likely to pick it up first thing in the morning.

In many ways, we shape our environment, and then our environment shapes us.

So, with that in mind, what does *your* default design look like?

Is it supporting your fundamentals? Is it helping you strengthen your circle of competence? Is it aligned with your why and the person you want to be?

The Activation Energy of Habits

At any given moment, the default effect is either working for you or against you. So, what you need to do is shape your environment to support the behaviors you want and discourage the behaviors you don't want.

A useful way of thinking about this is in terms of what psychology professor Mihaly Csikszentmihalyi refers to as the activation energy of habits.

The basic idea is this: the harder a behavior is to do, the more activation energy it needs, and the less likely you'll be to do it.

In his book *Finding Flow*, Csikszentmihalyi explains that "if a person is too tired, anxious, or lacks the discipline to overcome that initial obstacle, he or she will have to settle for something that, although less enjoyable, is more accessible." So, to change your habits, what you need to do is:

- decrease the activation energy of your desired behaviors (in other words, make them as easy as possible to do); and

- increase the activation energy of your undesired behaviors (in other words, make them as hard as possible to do).

Here are a few examples:

- If you want to sleep better, ban all screens from your bedroom and place a fiction book next to your bed.

- If you want to eat less, store your big plates and put salad plates in their place.

- If you want to learn more, replace entertainment and games with educational apps in your phone.

Shape Your Environment, Change Your Outcomes

According to behavior expert BJ Fogg: "There's just one way to radically change your behavior: radically change your environment."

If you make your desired habits very easy to do and unwanted behaviors very hard to do, you won't have to worry about self-discipline. You'll simply turn to the right behaviors by default.

Now, that is easier said than done, of course. If you're anything like me, you'll find yourself reverting to your unhelpful behaviors from time to time. My email app, for example, mysteriously tends to get reinstalled in my phone from time to time.

But if you stay mindful of your default design and keep adjusting it every time you fall back, you'll gradually get better at shaping your environment and changing your behavior.

STRATEGY #12: A QUICK SUMMARY

- A lot of what we do happens not because of *who* we are, but rather *where* we are.

- When we are presented with several options, we tend to choose the default one.

- You can change your habits by changing their activation energy—make desired behaviors easy to do and undesired behaviors hard to do.

Action Steps

Shape Your Environment to Match the Behaviors You Want

- ✔ Decrease the activation energy of your desired behaviors. Make your fundamental habits as easy as possible to do.

- ✔ Increase the activation energy of your undesired behaviors. Make competing behaviors as hard as possible to do.

STRATEGY #13

SURROUND YOURSELF WITH
THE RIGHT PEOPLE

Imagine sitting down at a table in a small room with seven other people. You're all about to participate in a psychology experiment on visual judgments.

The experimenter places two cards in front of you. The card on the left shows one vertical line. The card to the right has three lines of varying length.

The whole group is now asked, one at a time, to choose which of the three lines on the card to the right matches the length of the card to the left. The task is repeated several times with different cards.

At first, everything runs smoothly. You can quickly determine which line is the best match and so do all of the other participants.

But then, suddenly, the entire group unanimously chooses what is clearly the wrong line before it's your turn.

The experimenter turns to you. What would you say?

The Science of Conformity

As is often the case with psychology experiments, the experimenter has played a little trick on you.

In reality, you are the only participant. All the other people at the table are actors who have been instructed to give the wrong answer to some of the cards simultaneously.

It's not your visual judgment but your level of conformity to the rest of the group that's being tested.

This clever study is one of the most famous in psychology and was initially conducted by psychologist Solomon Asch. And the results were remarkable.

On average, about 33 percent of the participants who were placed in this situation conformed to the clearly incorrect majority. Over twelve attempts, about 75 percent conformed at least once.

How We Adapt to Other People

Human beings are social creatures. Our need for belonging is very strong. Apparently, it's so strong that we prefer giving an answer that is clearly wrong, as long as it makes us feel part of the group. And that tendency to adapt to the people around us has some serious practical implications for our lives. One study, for example, showed that if your friend becomes obese, your risk of obesity increases by 57 percent.

Social scientists are well aware of how much we affect each other. They know that humans have a strong tendency to adopt the same goals and even the same feelings as the people around them. Whether we realize it or not, the people around us determine what's normal. They set the standard for how we should think, feel and behave. If you hang out with people who are pessimistic and lazy, you're likely to feel as negative and perform as poorly as they do. But if you instead surround yourself with enthusiastic and hardworking people, those are the attributes you'll adopt.

Conduct Is Contagious

When I started getting into writing a few years ago, I'd almost always wait for inspiration to strike before I got to work. I'd publish very infrequently, and very few people would read my articles. But then, I started to connect with other writers. Pretty soon, I was adopting their routines and started writing every day. As a result, I published new material every week, and my audience began to grow.

These days, I'm surrounded by prolific writers and successful authors. As a result, I write more than ever before, my audience is in the thousands, and I've published two books.

And the fascinating part is that I hardly noticed it. The people around me established a new standard—a new "normal" way for me to think, feel, and act. And without consciously choosing to do so, I conformed to it.

That's the power of your social circles. And that's why you have to be very careful about who you let inside of them. The people around you will inevitably "infect" you with their beliefs, emotions, and goals. You can't immunize yourself to it—but you can choose who you allow to infect you.

STRATEGY #13: A QUICK SUMMARY

- Human beings are social creatures with a strong tendency to conform to each other.
- We adopt the goals, beliefs, feelings, and attitudes of those around us.
- Your social circles determine what's normal for you.
- You can't immunize yourself to conformity—but you can choose who you conform to.

Action Steps

Shape Your Social Circles

✔ Write down the names of at least three people you would like to conform to. If you can't think of anyone, list out the places, events, or online communities where you could connect with these people.

✔ Establish at least one of the following:

1. An accountability partnership. Connect with one person regularly to talk about specific goals you're pursuing. Hold each other accountable to daily or weekly actions.

2. A coaching relationship. Hire a personal coach to help raise your standards and hold you accountable. You can find a list of great coaches here.

3. A mastermind group. Put together a group of 3–5 people with similar goals. Meet up in person or online for an hour once a week to give each other feedback and encouragement.

4. A mentorship. Find someone who is further down the path you want to pursue and let that person guide you.

STRATEGY #14

PLAY POORLY WELL

Jack Nicklaus is widely regarded as one of the greatest golf players of all time.

During his career, he won eighteen major championships, while producing nineteen second-places and nine third-places over a period of twenty-five years.

In his book *The Secret of Golf*, sports journalist Joe Posnanski recounts Nicklaus's opinion on what makes a golf player great: "I have always felt that the mettle of a player is not how well he plays when he's playing well, but how well he scores and plays when he's playing poorly."

No matter what you're trying to achieve, that is a key idea to keep in mind. Let me explain why.

The Crucial Skill of Playing Poorly Well

We all know what it's like to work on our goals when we're feeling inspired, everything is running smoothly, and we're making big progress. Those moments will never be a problem. Anyone can take action when things are going well.

What separates remarkably successful people is their ability to get things done at all times. They show up and do the work even when they're uninspired, everything is going against them, and they keep getting stuck.

In other words, they know how to play poorly well. And that gives them a huge advantage in life because it allows them to preserve their momentum.

The Power of Momentum

We tend to think of our habits in a vacuum: "If I skip the gym today, it won't make much of a difference in my long-term results." And although that is true, it doesn't account for the importance of momentum.

If you skip one day, you might as well skip two. If one day off doesn't affect your results, two days won't either. And once you've skipped two days, you might as well skip the rest of the week. It still won't affect the results much. Plus, you'll get a fresh start on Monday, right?

Well, not really. Because once your momentum is gone, it will be much harder to get back into your routine. It might take you weeks, months, or even years to get going again.

And that is why, on any given day, your results aren't that important. What is much more important is that you keep your momentum going.

Always Keep Big Mo Happy

In his book *The Compound Effect*, Darren Hardy refers to momentum as his friend, "Big Mo." Hardy elaborates on Big Mo on his Facebook page:

> You can't see or feel Mo, but you know when you've got it. You can't count on Mo showing up to every occasion, but when it does – WOW! Big Mo can catapult you into the stratosphere

of success. And once you've got Mo on your side, there's almost no way anyone can catch you!

In my experience, it only takes a couple of slipups to scare off this precious friend. If you miss one day, Mo gets cranky. If you miss two days, he's packing his bags. And if you miss three days, he leaves and won't be back for a long time.

Big Mo can help you achieve more than you ever thought possible. So, you should be kind to him. You should strive to keep him happy at all times. How?

In Case of Emergency: Bring Out the Tomato Cans

Do you remember the tomato cans from strategy #6? You know, the minimum daily targets that are so easy you're pretty much guaranteed to win? Well, it turns out that Big Mo *loves* them. So, whenever you feel like you're not on top of your game, revert to your tomato cans. Forget about the long-term results and instead focus on keeping your momentum going.

Doing that has two significant benefits. First, it keeps Big Mo happy. You'll ensure you won't have to start over without him. Second, it reduces overwhelm. Once you've knocked over a tomato can, you'll often find that you want to keep going. Getting started is almost always the hardest part. So, by aiming for an easy target, you can "trick" yourself into a much greater effort.

That's how you turn a poor effort into a good one. It's how you play poorly well.

STRATEGY #14: A QUICK SUMMARY

- No matter what you're trying to achieve, you need to be able to play poorly well.

- What separates remarkably successful people is their ability to show up and do the work even when they're uninspired, everything is going against them, and they keep getting stuck.

- On any given day, your results aren't that important. What is much more important is that you keep your momentum. At all times, keep Big Mo happy!

Action Steps

Return to Your Tomato Cans

- ✔ Keep your momentum by reverting to minimum daily targets that are so easy you're pretty much guaranteed to win. If you want, you can mark these occasions with the letter T for "tomato can" in the chain in your calendar.

STRATEGY #15

BE KIND TO YOURSELF

We've covered a lot of strategies in this book. But, as I've mentioned before, the only way to discover how powerful they are, is to implement them in your own life. And as you go about doing that, you're going to mess up from time to time. It doesn't matter how solid your fundamentals are or how many strategies you put to use. There will inevitably be setbacks, challenges, and losses. And when they happen, the way you deal with them is going to be crucial to your success.

Self-Criticism Isn't Helpful

"You're so lazy. You'll never get this done. You're such a failure."

These are some prime examples of things we would never say to other people. And yet, we usually have no problem saying them to ourselves.

When it comes to motivating other people, we understand that harsh criticism won't be helpful. But when it comes to motivating ourselves, our attitude is different. For some reason, we think that we need to be hard on ourselves to achieve our goals. And that's a big problem not only because heavy self-criticism makes us feel bad but also because it makes us much less likely to achieve our goals.

So, instead of being your own worst enemy, become your own best friend. Stop bringing yourself down and start lifting yourself up. Instead of criticizing, offer yourself compassion.

The Science of Self-Compassion

The research field of self-compassion is relatively new to Western psychology, but the concept itself has been around in Buddhist thought for a long time.

Dr. Kristin Neff is a pioneering researcher in the field. In her book *Self-Compassion*, she defines the term as "extending compassion to one's self in instances of perceived inadequacy, failure, or general suffering":

> Instead of mercilessly judging and criticizing yourself for various inadequacies or shortcomings, self-compassion means you are kind and understanding when confronted with personal failings—after all, who ever said you were supposed to be perfect?

According to Neff's definition, self-compassion consists of three elements:

1) **Mindfulness.** Holding one's painful thoughts and feelings in mindful awareness rather than avoiding them or over-identifying with them.

2) **Common humanity.** Seeing one's fallibility as part of the larger human condition rather than personal shortcomings.

3) **Self-kindness.** Being kind and understanding toward oneself rather than being self-critical.

Researchers have found that treating yourself with compassion brings many benefits, including the following:

- **Less anxiety and depression.** A key feature of self-compassion is the lack of self-criticism, and self-criticism is a big predictor of anxiety and depression.

- **Increased productivity.** A high level of self-compassion among students is associated with less procrastination and greater motivation to complete assignments.

- **Greater creativity.** Self-judgmental people demonstrate greater "creative originality" after practicing self-compassion exercises.

- **Better self-regulation.** Smokers, who offered themselves self-compassion rather than self-condemnation, were better able to cut down on their smoking.

- **Improved relationships.** Self-compassionate partners are described by their partners as being more emotionally connected and accepting and less detached, controlling, and aggressive than those lacking self-compassion.

So, despite what many people think, self-criticism won't create self-discipline. If you want to feel great and perform at your very best, you need self-compassion.

How to Cultivate Self-Compassion

Whenever you feel the impulse to be self-critical, remember that stacking shame and guilt on top of what you consider a poor performance only makes it harder to bounce back. Being hard on yourself is neither healthy nor productive.

So, practice self-compassion instead. Neff recommends you use a mantra that guides you through the three elements of self-compassion (mindfulness, common humanity, and self-kindness). Put your hands on your heart, feel the warmth and gentle touch of your hands on your chest. Then say to yourself:

1. "This is a moment of suffering."

That's the mindfulness element. Other alternatives are:

- "This is painful."
- "Ouch."
- "This is hard."

2. "Suffering is part of life."

That's the common humanity element. Other alternatives are:

- "Other people also feel like this."
- "I'm not alone in this."
- "Everyone feels this way this sometimes."

3. "May I be kind to myself."

That's the self-kindness element. Other alternatives are:

- "May I give myself the support I need."
- "May I accept myself just the way I am."
- "May I forgive myself for this."

These sentences are just suggestions. Use them as inspiration to create a mantra in your own words. What's important is that you find a phrasing that includes the three elements of self-compassion and that it feels right for you.

STRATEGY #15: A QUICK SUMMARY

- There will inevitably be setbacks, challenges, and losses. How you deal with them when they happen is crucial for your success.
- Self-criticism brings you down. It makes you feel bad and decreases your ability to achieve your goals.

- Self-compassion lifts you up. It makes you feel good and increases your ability to achieve your goals.

- Self-compassion consists of three elements: mindfulness, common humanity, and self-kindness.

Action Steps

Practice Self-Compassion

✔ Create a self-compassion mantra that includes mindfulness, common humanity, and self-kindness.

✔ Whenever you have a setback, place your hands on your heart, feel the gentle touch and warmth on your chest, and repeat the mantra to yourself.

FINAL THOUGHTS ON DEVELOPING SELF-DISCIPLINE

We're approaching the end of our journey together. But before you close this book and go put your habits and strategies into action in your life, I'd like to share one final idea with you.

In 1995, film studio Pixar released *Toy Story*—the first computer-animated feature film. Since then, the studio has produced sixteen more movies, including titles like *A Bug's Life*, *Monsters, Inc.*, *Finding Nemo*, *The Incredibles*, *Cars*, *Ratatouille*, and *WALL-E*. That list of blockbusters has earned Pixar sixteen Academy Awards, seven Golden Globe Awards, eleven Grammy Awards and a bunch of other awards and acknowledgments.

In his book, *Little Bets*, Peter Sims explain that there is a lot we can learn from how Pixar goes about creating its exceptional movies.

From Suck to Unsuck

We tend to think brilliant companies like Pixar always know exactly what to do next. Presumably, the studio's workflow looks something like this:

1) One of their genius employees comes up with a brilliant idea.

2) The genius employee explains the brilliant idea to the rest of the uber-talented team.

3) The uber-talented team executes flawlessly to turn the genius employee's brilliant idea into an amazing blockbuster movie.

But in reality, that's not at all how it works. The truth is that each of Pixar's movies goes through a process of relentless iteration before it's finished.

Sure, an initial idea gets the project moving, but it will change many times before the film is released. In fact, Pixar assumes that the first versions of its movies are going to suck.

And as a result, Pixar is willing to tweak everything about them until they don't suck anymore. Their process is all about going from suck to unsuck.

A Mountain of Storyboards

For each movie that it creates, Pixar uses thousands of storyboards. These are hand-drawn comic book versions of the film that contain ideas for the characters and actions they take in each scene.

The people working on the project come up with a huge number of these ideas, most of which are never used in the final product. And the number of storyboards they use increases for each successful movie they release. So far, they've created:

- 27,565 storyboards for *A Bug's Life*;
- 43,536 storyboards for *Finding Nemo*;
- 69,562 storyboards for *Ratatouille*;
- 98,173 storyboards for *WALL-E*.

Clearly, Pixar has no intention of slowing down its iterations. And here's my point: neither should you.

How Good Intentions Fizzle Out

We all tend to think that the changes we want to create in our lives should play out exactly the way we imagine. If we just come up with a solid enough plan, we should be able to follow through without major problems.

And that might be true for a week or two. But then it turns out that our plan has a hole or two (or a hundred). Perhaps we notice that we don't have enough energy to show up at the gym after work consistently. Or that the book we planned to read is boring. Or that there just isn't enough time to prepare the healthy food we've been planning. And so, we lose momentum (bye-bye, Big Mo), our good intentions fizzle out, and we quit, feeling helpless and discouraged.

Always Be Creating Storyboards

If you can relate to this frustrating cycle, the problem is not that you're lazy or lack self-discipline. The problem is that you rely too much on the first version of your plan.

You overestimate your ability to predict every obstacle that will show up in your way. As a result, each time you run into a setback, you'll perceive it as a failure and get discouraged.

And here's why Pixar's approach is so powerful. Instead of thinking of your first plan as your definitive strategy, it becomes your first draft. You'll assume that it's going to have holes. Probably plenty of them. In fact, your plan is probably going to suck.

That approach allows you to face setbacks without getting discouraged. You know that your plan is a work in progress, so every time you run into an obstacle, you simply create a new "storyboard." And for each one you create, you move closer to unsuck.

Here's a powerful "brain tattoo":

There's No Failure, Only Feedback

Just because you've failed a lot in the past doesn't mean you're a failure. It just means you've created a lot of storyboards.

And that's actually a good thing because it means you have a lot of insights into what hasn't worked in the past. Now all you have to do is create a new storyboard and try again. If that doesn't work, you create a new one and try again. And again. And again. And again.

Continuously refine your plan by revisiting and tweaking the habits and strategies in this book until they work for you. The only way to fail is to quit. So, refuse to do that.

Build Your Mountain of Storyboards

Pixar was willing to make 98,173 storyboards to create *WALL-E*. And it will continue to make even more for its future films. Pixar doesn't waste its time worrying about setbacks. And neither should you.

The question isn't if you have what it takes. The question is: How many storyboards are you willing to create?

As long as you do not stop, you are succeeding. What will your next storyboard look like?

GRAB YOUR FREE WORKBOOK

You've made it to the end of this book. Great job reading all the way through! If you're excited to start working on the habits and strategies suggested, I highly recommend downloading your copy of *The Self-Discipline Blueprint Workbook* right now.

https://patrikedblad.com/the-good-life-blueprint-series-bonuses

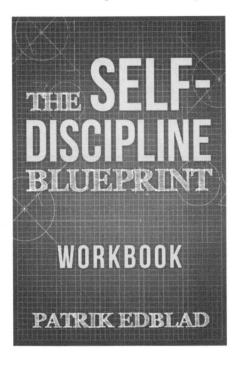

This resource will take you through everything we've covered step-by-step and make it as easy as possible for you to implement everything you've learned.

BOOK 3

THE DECISION-MAKING BLUEPRINT

A SIMPLE GUIDE TO
BETTER CHOICES
IN LIFE AND WORK

PATRIK EDBLAD

YOUR FREE BONUS BUNDLE

We'll be covering a lot of powerful concepts in this book. To make it as easy as possible for you to internalize them and use them in your decision-making, this companion resource contains:

- 3 beautiful posters that outline all the cognitive biases, logical fallacies, and mental models covered in the book.
- 45 handy flash cards to help you learn all these concepts by heart.
- A simple checklist of mental models for you to use every time you make an important decision.

Go here to grab *The Decision-Making Blueprint Bonus Bundle*
https://patrikedblad.com/the-good-life-blueprint-series-bonuses

CONTENTS

PART 1: INTRODUCTION

You cannot change your destination overnight,
but you can change direction overnight.

—Jim Rohn

The Secrets to Great Decision-Making

Throughout history, standard economic theory was dominated by the model of "homo economicus": the economic man. According to that model, humans are self-interested, intelligent, and analytical beings who can control their feelings and impulses. The economic man constantly evaluates all the facts, weighs the costs and benefits, and makes rational decisions to maximize personal well-being.

This view of humans as cold and rational calculators provides a convenient foundation for economic theories.

The only problem? No such person exists.

The Fall of Homo Economicus

It turns out that people often make decisions that don't deliver the best outcomes. Sometimes, we even make choices that we know will hurt our future prospects.

The first researchers to study these peculiar tendencies extensively were psychologists Daniel Kahneman and Amos Tversky. In the early 1970s, they started investigating the psychology involved in decision-making and running experiments to test their hypotheses.

Over the coming years, they compiled a long list of well-documented irrational behaviors, and in 1979 they published their key paper, "Prospect Theory: An Analysis of Decision Under Risk."[1]

Their findings caused a lot of controversy, especially among economists looking to protect their worldview. But Kahneman and Tversky stood their ground, and their work eventually marked the start for a new field of study.

The Rise of Behavioral Economics

Behavioral economics is a subfield of economics that studies how psychological, social, and emotional factors influence decision-making. The fundamental principle of this discipline is that people make systematic errors in their thinking.

Behavioral economists have found that the vast majority of our choices aren't the result of careful calculations. Instead, we rely heavily on mental shortcuts like rules of thumb, intuition, and common sense to form judgments, solve problems, and make decisions.

These shortcuts can work well in a lot of situations but, at times, they also result in cognitive biases and logical fallacies, thinking errors that distort our reasoning and derail our judgment.

An Ancient Brain in a Modern World

So, why do we make systematic errors in our thinking? Why do we use mental shortcuts instead of carefully calculating our decisions? What makes us susceptible to biases and fallacies?

The answers to those questions lie in our evolutionary past. Our brains have evolved for millions of years, not to maximize our well-being, but to keep us alive.

For most of our history, we lived in an environment that was wildly different from modern society. And that explains why we reason the way we do.

Mental shortcuts provided an efficient means for us to make quick decisions with limited knowledge in a complex world.

A lot of decisions that seem irrational today served us well in the environment we evolved in. To illustrate that, let's have a look at an example.

Loss Aversion

People have a tendency to prefer avoiding losses to acquiring equivalent gains. In other words, we feel better not losing $10 than we do finding $10.

Some research suggests that losses are twice as powerful, psychologically, as gains. And from an evolutionary perspective, that's a useful mechanism.

For most of human history, reductions in resources could lead to death. In that scenario, it makes sense to place a higher value on preventing losses than obtaining gains.

In modern-day life, however, losses rarely have the same dire consequences. And since that's the case, loss aversion no longer makes rational sense.

In the past, loss aversion helped our ancestors protect their scarce resources and stay alive. But in the present, the same bias often leads to poor decisions. When investing, for example, most people keep losing stocks and sell winning stocks even though, rationally, they should do the exact opposite.

Bad Decisions Everywhere

Loss aversion is just one example of how the brain makes systematic errors. There are many other biases and fallacies that diminish our ability to make sound judgments and reason logically.

We are fundamentally wired for mistakes and, as a result, we make a lot of poor decisions. The evidence is everywhere.

Career choices, for instance, are often regretted or abandoned. According to a Gallup report,[2] a majority of Americans would change at least one education decision, including their choice of college, their major, or their degree, if they could do it all over again.

When it comes to our health, we consistently make choices that are bad for us. One in three adults doesn't get enough sleep.[3] Roughly the same number of people are physically inactive.[4] And out of all deaths worldwide, 20 percent are attributable to bad food choices.[5]

We don't do much better in our social lives. Young people frequently start relationships with people who are bad for them. About 40 to 50 percent of marriages end in divorce.[6] And at the end of life, some of the most common regrets are working too much and losing touch with friends.[7]

The reason we struggle so much in these areas, and many others, is that we lack decision-making skills. Despite the vast implications our choices have on our lives, we're never explicitly taught how to make them.

A Simple Guide to Great Thinking

The good news is that you can train your brain to think in new and better ways. And in this book, I will show you exactly how to do that. In the chapters ahead, you'll discover:

- The cognitive biases that distort your thinking, and how to counteract them.
- The logical fallacies that derail your judgment, and how to prevent them.

- The mental models you need to equip your mind with to make great decisions.

We'll draw from philosophical ideas, psychological research, and powerful concepts from a wide variety of disciplines so you can deeply understand and consistently improve the cognitive apparatus of your mind.

By the end of this book, you'll have a solid foundation for rational, logical, and effective thinking. As a result, you'll make smarter decisions and get better outcomes than ever before.

And if any of this sounds complicated—don't worry. Everything is explained in a clear and simple way. I'll take your hand and guide you every step of the way. All you have to do is follow along, absorb, and apply the concepts to your own thinking.

Your Decisions Shape Your Life

Each day, from the instant you wake up until the moment you fall asleep, you are making countless choices.

Some decisions are big: "What career should I pursue?," "Where should I live?," "Should I get married or not?" These choices are defining moments we know will have a significant impact on our lives.

Most decisions are small: "Should I get up or hit the snooze button?," "What should I have for lunch?," "Should I take the stairs or the elevator?" These choices might not matter much in the moment, but over time, they will compound into striking results.

So, to get desirable outcomes in life, you need to make good decisions—both big and small. Good decisions repeated over time lead to success. Bad decisions repeated over time lead to failure.

The choices you've made until now have brought you where you are right now. And the decisions you make going forward will determine the life you'll lead in the future.

Change Your Trajectory

If you read and implement what you learn in this book, I promise that you'll radically improve your decision-making skills.

You'll be able to spot the inherent mental errors and reasoning flaws in your mind. And you'll be able to use a wide variety of thinking tools to understand reality and solve problems.

In short, you'll think better. And that will allow you to experience the satisfaction of making great decisions and, ultimately, the fulfillment of shaping the life you want.

So, make a life-changing decision right now and keep on reading. Your future self will be happy you did.

On the next page, we'll have a quick look at how to best use this book. Then we'll get right into the good stuff as I lay out the Decision-Making Blueprint.

Let's dive in!

How to Use This Book

The Decision-Making Blueprint is divided into five parts. Right now you're reading part 1, which is the introduction. Next, in part 2, we'll examine the cognitive biases that distort your thinking and how to counteract them. Then, in part 3, we'll explore the logical fallacies that derail your judgment and how to prevent them. After that, in part 4, we'll equip your mind with the mental models you need to make great decisions. And lastly, in part 5, I'll share some final words on how to improve your decision-making skills continuously.

This book contains everything you need to improve your thinking, make smarter decisions, and get better results. But that will only happen if you move from theory to practice. So, commit right now to using the concepts in your everyday life right away.

As you're making choices, reflect on the cognitive biases that might influence your thinking. When you're talking to others, pay attention to the logical fallacies that show up. And whenever you're making an important decision, use the mental models at your disposal.

To make all of that as easy as possible, I recommend you download *The Decision-Making Blueprint Bonus Bundle*. The posters, flash cards, and checklist will make everything you're learning much simpler to internalize and put to use.

Are you ready? Let's get started!

PART 2: COGNITIVE BIASES

The mind of man at one and the same time is both the glory and the shame of the universe.

—Blaise Pascal

The Mental Errors That Distort Your Thinking

It's been estimated that the human brain can make roughly a billion billion calculations per second. That's far more than any computer that exists today.

In fact, it took one of the world's most powerful supercomputers—housing 705,024 processor cores and 1.4 million gigabytes of RAM—40 minutes to simulate just one second of thinking.[8]

But despite its impressive capacity, the brain still makes systematic mistakes.

Cognitive Biases

We all have inherent thinking errors in the way we perceive, process, and interpret information from the world around us.

Psychologists refer to these errors as cognitive biases: "a systematic pattern of deviation from norm or rationality in judgment."[9]

The world is an extremely complicated place, and cognitive biases are often a result of your brain's attempt to simplify the input it's receiving. And that's not necessarily a bad thing. Cognitive biases help us act fast, filter information, construct meaning, and remember what's important.

But they can also be problematic. At times, they lead to perceptual distortions, inaccurate judgment, and irrational decisions.

A fascinating study by researchers Eric Johnson and Daniel Goldstein[10] provides a great example of how cognitive bias can affect our choices—without us even realizing it. Let's have a look at it next.

Would You Like to Be an Organ Donor?

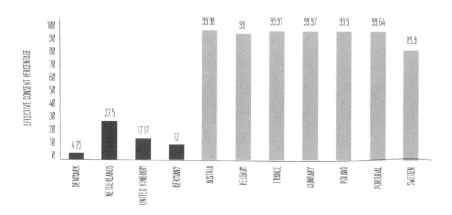

EFFECTIVE CONSENT RATES, BY COUNTRY. EXPLICIT CONSENT (OPT-IN, GOLD) AND PRESUMED CONSENT (OPT-OUT, BLUE)

This graph shows the percentage of people across several European countries who are willing to donate their organs after they die.

Note the massive difference between the countries on the left and the ones on the right. Why do you think that is?

At first glance, you might assume some major underlying factor like culture or religion caused these results, but at a closer look, that doesn't hold up.

Denmark and Sweden, the Netherlands and Belgium, Austria and Germany—these are all countries with similar cultures and religious beliefs.

Still, their organ donation percentages are wildly different. What's really going on here?

The Default Effect

What explains the differences between the countries is the design of the form related to organ donations in each region.

213

In the countries where the form has an "opt-in" design (i.e., "Check this box if you want to donate your organs"), people tend not to check the box.

And in the countries where the form has an "opt-out" design (i.e., "Check this box if you don't want to donate your organs"), people also tend not to check the box.

No matter which one of these forms people are presented with, an overwhelming majority of them will choose the default option.

When you decide whether to donate your organs, you may feel like you're making a deliberate choice. But in reality, you're much more likely to choose whatever is presented as the standard choice.

This is known as the default effect, and it's just one example of how cognitive biases can affect our decisions. In the upcoming pages, we'll cover many more.

Debiasing

It's important to note that you can't completely rid yourself of cognitive biases. That's not possible, nor desirable. As we've seen, cognitive biases have evolved for a reason. They are hardwired into your brain because you need them to navigate the world.

But what you can do is use debiasing to reduce the influence of biases in your judgment and decisions. That can be very helpful, especially when it comes to particularly important decisions.

So, in the chapters ahead, we'll look at the most common cognitive biases related to decision-making and what you can do to decrease their effects.

And we'll begin with the granddaddy of them all...

1. CONFIRMATION BIAS

*Our tendency to favor information that
confirms our existing beliefs.*

Imagine that you're participating in a psychology experiment. The experimenter gives you a three number sequence and informs you that these numbers follow a particular rule only she knows about.

Your task is to figure out what that rule is, and you can do that by proposing your own three number strings and asking the experimenter whether or not they meet the rule. The series of numbers you're given is:

2-4-6

Try it! What underlying rule do you think these numbers follow? And what's another string you can give to the experimenter to see if you're right?

If you're like most people, you'll assume the rule is "numbers increasing by two" or "ascending even numbers." To find out if you're right, you guess something like:

10-12-14

And to your delight, the experimenter says, "Yes, that string of numbers follows the rule." To make sure that your hypothesis is correct, you propose another sequence:

50-52-54

"Yes!" the experimenter says, and you confidently make your guess about the underlying rule: "Even numbers, ascending in twos!" To your surprise, the experimenter says "No!"

It turns out that the rule is "any ascending numbers." So, 10-12-14 and 50-52-54 fit the rule, but so does 1-2-3 or 9-748-1047.

The only way to figure that out is to guess strings of numbers that would prove your beloved hypothesis wrong—and that's not something that comes naturally to us. In the original study,[11] only one in five participants guessed the correct rule.

The 2-4-6 task beautifully illustrates our bias toward confirming, rather than disproving, our ideas. And that tendency has a massive influence on how we interpret information, form beliefs, and make decisions.

Consider, for example, the global warming controversy. Let's say Mary believes climate change is a serious issue. Because of that, she seeks out and reads stories about how the climate is changing. As a result, she continues to confirm and support those beliefs.

Meanwhile, Linda does not believe that climate change is a serious issue. Because of that, she seeks out and reads stories about how climate change is a hoax. As a result, she continues to confirm and support those beliefs instead.

The confirmation bias makes us pay attention to what supports our views and dismiss what doesn't. And the more convinced we become about something, the more we'll filter out and ignore all evidence to the contrary.

It feels much better to support our beliefs than it does to discredit them. Evaluating and adjusting our worldview is scary, uncomfortable, and strenuous. So we prefer strengthening it instead.

The confirmation bias helps us do that. But it does so at the expense of clear judgment. To keep an open, flexible, and rational mind, you have to continually challenge what you think you know.

You need to deliberately seek out disconfirming evidence and always be ready to change your mind. It's not easy but, with practice, it will make you much better at interpreting information, updating your beliefs, and making well-informed decisions.

2. SELF-SERVING BIAS

*Our tendency to take credit for successes
and deny responsibility for failures.*

"If it worked, it was because of me. If it didn't, it was because of someone or something else." This kind of reasoning takes place all the time and, on a psychological level, it makes sense. We all feel a need to protect and build our self-esteem, and the self-serving bias helps us do that.

Imagine, for example, that you're trying to get your driver's license. If you pass your driving test on the first try, you'll probably think it happened because of your excellent driving skills. But if you fail, you'll likely blame it on the incompetent examiner, the awful car, the bad weather or, well, pretty much anything else other than your own performance.

Studies on the self-serving bias have found that it shows up in a wide variety of situations, including:

- School–If a student gets a good grade, it's because of his hard work and intelligence. But if he gets a bad grade, it's because of the poor teacher or the unfair test.[12]

- Work–If a job applicant gets hired, it's because of her qualifications. But if she doesn't, it's because the interviewer didn't like her.[13]

- Sports–If a team wins a game, it's because of practice and skill. But if they lose, it's because of the referee.[14]

We also consistently make what psychologists refer to as the "fundamental attribution error." When other people make mistakes, we blame the person. But when we make mistakes ourselves, we blame the circumstances.

Let's say you've gotten your driver's license (thanks to your excellent driving skills, of course), and you're cruising down the highway when, suddenly, somebody passes you going well over the speed limit. In this scenario, you'll likely conclude that the other driver is a reckless jerk.

But if the roles were reversed, and you're the one driving too fast, you'd probably blame the circumstances instead. Unlike other drivers, you're not some irresponsible maniac. If you're speeding, it's because the situation, perhaps an emergency, warranted it.

With these tendencies in mind, it's no surprise we also rate ourselves more positively than others. Research on what psychologists call "illusory superiority" shows that most of us consider ourselves better than average in school, at work, in social settings, and in many other situations.

Reasoning this way feels good. It helps us save face, hang on to our self-esteem, and avoid hurtful emotions like shame. But it also prevents our learning and growth. If you blame your failures on the circumstances, there's not much you can do about it. But if you accept responsibility for them, you can improve and do better next time.

So be mindful of your tendency to irrationally protect your self-esteem. When you experience setbacks, resist the urge to pass the blame and take ownership instead. Don't ask "Whose fault is this?" but "What can I learn from this?" That way, you can continually course-correct, make wiser decisions, and get better results.

3. AVAILABILITY BIAS

Our tendency to base our judgments on
what most easily springs to mind.

If you're like most people, you consume the morning news with a sense of anxiety and fear. Each day, we read about shootings, war, and the spread of nuclear weapons. It's no wonder most of us feel like the world is getting increasingly worse.

But the truth is that we are actually living in the least violent time in history. In his book *The Better Angels of Our Nature*,[15] psychologist Steven Pinker shows that the numbers of homicides, armed conflicts, and nuclear weapons are all actually declining.

Most people have a hard time accepting these statistics. Some even refuse to believe them. If this is the most peaceful time in history, then why are there so many reports of murders? Why does everyone keep talking about wars? And why do we hear about nuclear weapons all the time?

The answer is that we are living in the most reported time in history. Information about horrifying stories from all over the world is more easily accessible than ever before. So, while the likelihood of dangerous events is going down, the chance that you'll hear about them is going up.

And this is where the availability bias comes into play. When an event springs easily to mind, our brain will exaggerate the frequency and magnitude of it. We constantly overestimate the impact of stuff we remember and underestimate the things we don't hear about. In the words of Daniel Kahneman:

"People tend to assess the relative importance of issues by the ease with which they are retrieved from memory—and this is largely determined by the extent of coverage in the media."[16]

The availability bias makes us bad at assessing risks and estimating probabilities. And that, in turn, affects our feelings, decisions, and outcomes. For example:

- If we hear about a plane crash, we might develop a fear of flying that severely limits the places we can travel.

- If we're told about a shark attack, we might avoid the ocean every time we're at the beach.

- If someone in our neighborhood wins the lottery, we might waste a lot of money on tickets.

The chances of experiencing a plane crash, getting attacked by a shark, or winning the grand prize in a lottery are tiny. But the brain doesn't care about that. Instead, it bases its immediate judgments on the vividness of the stories we're told about these events.

To make well-informed decisions, you need to keep this tendency in mind. Whenever you're presented with news and stories, try to recall instances of the event that aren't so memorable. For example, ask yourself how many people you know who have:

- Not died in a plane crash?

- Never been attacked by a shark?

- Failed to win the lottery jackpot?

Or do a quick Google search and look up the real-world probabilities for these events. That way, you can keep the availability bias in check, minimize unnecessary stress, and avoid irrational decisions.

4. SURVIVORSHIP BIAS

*Our tendency to focus on things that "survive" a
process while overlooking those that don't.*

During World War II, the British military was losing their bombers at an alarming rate. As they were flying over enemy territory, they were being shot down so often that they decided to add armor to their planes.

But they couldn't shield the entire surface of their aircraft. That would make them too heavy to take off. So they decided to put the armor in the most critical places.

To find out what those areas were, they carefully investigated the aircraft that came back from battle and noted where they had been damaged the most. The investigators found that the majority of the bullet holes were on the wings, around the tail gunner, and down the center of the body.

Now, let's imagine that you were in charge of the investigation. With that information at your disposal, where would you put the armor?

Most likely, you would want to do what the real commanders planned on doing. They wanted to shield the parts that had the most bullet holes: the wings, the tail gunner, and the center of the body.

It seems like the obvious choice, but it would have been a terrible idea. Why? Remember, the investigators had only considered the aircrafts that *survived* their missions. None of the planes that had been shot down had been taken into account.

The holes in the examined aircraft represented the areas where the bombers could take damage and still make it home. Counterintuitively, it was the unharmed parts of the examined planes that needed the armor. Because if those were hit, the aircraft would be lost, and it wouldn't show up in the investigation.

Luckily for the British military, statistician Abraham Wald pointed that out and helped them avoid a crucial mistake.[17] But in everyday life, we fall for the survivorship bias all the time, and it has significant implications on our judgment and decisions.

Consider, for example, the famous stories of how successful people like Richard Branson, Bill Gates, and Mark Zuckerberg all dropped out of school. Learning about them, many people conclude that you don't need a college education to succeed.

But for every Branson, Gates, and Zuckerberg, there are thousands, if not millions, of other entrepreneurs who dropped out of school and failed in business. We just don't hear about them, and so we don't take them into account.

When you pay attention to the winners and ignore the losers, it's difficult to say if a particular strategy will be successful. So whenever you're presented with a success story, ask yourself if it provides a complete picture, or if it's only taking survivors into account. That way, you'll make more accurate judgments and avoid costly mistakes.

5. LOSS AVERSION

Our tendency to prefer avoiding losses
to acquiring equivalent gains.

Imagine that I invite you to play a game right now. The rules are simple. We'll flip a coin. If it shows heads, you'll lose $100. And if it shows tails, you'll win $100. Would you take that bet?

If you're like most people, you wouldn't. And since the risk and reward of the bet are precisely the same, that makes sense. So, let's change the rules a little. If it shows heads, you'll still lose $100. But if it shows tails, you'll now win $110. Would you take the bet this time?

Interestingly, most people would still not want to play. The game has a positive expected value of 10 percent, meaning that, on average, you'll win $10 every time you play. But that doesn't matter. Psychologically, the risk of losing our hard-earned $100 outweighs the potential reward.

Sure, we enjoy winning. But we really, really hate losing. And that leads to poor reasoning and silly decisions.

In fact, when researchers offer people the chance to play the coin flip game, they find that most of us demand a chance to win $200 or more to participate. And that, in the words of Daniel Kahneman, is "ridiculously loss averse."[18]

A major implication of loss aversion is something called the "endowment effect," our tendency to perceive things as more valuable just because we own them. To understand how it works, let's have a look at another experiment.

In this study,[19] the researchers took a big group of students and split them into two groups. They gave the first group a mug and asked, "For how much would you sell your mug?" and "How much would you pay for a candy bar?" Then they gave the second group a candy bar and asked, "For how much would you sell your candy bar?" and "How much would you pay for a mug?"

Since they gave out the mugs and candy randomly, you would expect that many people would prefer the other item. But that's not at all the case. What you'll find when you do this experiment is that almost no one switches.

The people who get mugs suddenly think mugs are amazing. And the people who get candy bars now think candy is terrific. Both groups end up valuing their item more highly and sticking to what they already have.

Loss aversion and the endowment effect makes us overprotect and overvalue what we have. And that often lead to choices, big and small, that are not in our best interest. It can make you hang on to losing stocks that ruin your portfolio, and it can make you keep needless possessions that clutter your house.

So whenever you feel anxious about a potential loss, compare the downside to the upside. Then dare to make the decision that makes rational sense, even if it feels uncomfortable. Over the long run, that will lead to much better results.

6. STATUS QUO BIAS

Our tendency to prefer that things stay as they already are.

In the early 1980s, Coca-Cola was on the edge of losing the cola war to their rivals Pepsi. The previous fifteen years, Coke's market share had remained flat while Pepsi's climbed steadily. To make matters worse, more and more consumers were switching to diet soft drinks and non-cola beverages.

So Coca-Cola decided to do something drastic. They started experimenting with their original formula. A new recipe was put forth, and it seemed very promising. Blind taste tests showed people liked the new formula more than regular Coke *and* Pepsi by a large margin.

In 1985, they launched the new and improved version of their drink. But despite the test results, the response from the public was extremely negative. After being bombarded by phone calls, 40,000 letters, and tons of bad press, the company reintroduced its original formula within three months.

Interestingly, the return of "Coca-Cola Classic" resulted in a significant increase in sales. That made some people speculate that introducing the new formula was a marketing ploy to stimulate sales of the original drink. The Coca-Cola Company, however, maintains that it was a genuine attempt to replace the original product.

Regardless, the introduction of the new Coke recipe is an excellent example of the status quo bias.[20] We like things the way they already are, so we treat any changes to the current state of affairs with a lot of skepticism and resistance.

That tendency can partly be explained by loss aversion and the endowment effect. We weigh the potential losses of switching from the status quo more heavily than the potential gains. But several other tendencies also contributes to the status quo bias, including:

- Psychological commitment–We want to justify previous actions and maintain a consistent self-image.

- Mere exposure–We prefer certain things just because they are familiar to us.

- Regret avoidance–We feel worse about bad decisions than we do about poor outcomes from inaction.

All of these tendencies can have big impacts on our decisions. Do you remember the organ donor study[21] a few chapters back? The status quo bias explains why people are inclined to stick with the default option. It's also why we tend to, for example:

- Go to the same restaurant, sit in the same spot, and order the same dish.

- Stick with the same internet, phone, and TV providers.

- Use the same bank, savings options, and insurance companies.

And there's nothing inherently wrong with any of those choices. In fact, the status quo bias can help us save energy and prevent unnecessary risks. But it can also make us miss out on great opportunities.

So whenever you feel like turning down a new choice, ask yourself why that is. Is your default option truly better, or are you being swayed by the comfort of the status quo?

7. ANCHORING BIAS

Our tendency to rely too much on an initial piece of information.

Imagine that you're out shopping, and as you walk into a clothing store, you spot a jacket you like. You try it on, check yourself out in the mirror, and decide you have to have it. Now, imagine the following two scenarios:

1) You check the price tag, and the jacket is $500. But a salesperson walks by and says, *"I'm sorry. That price is wrong. The jacket is really $300."*

2) You check the price tag, and the jacket is $100. But a salesperson walks by and says, *"I'm sorry. That price is wrong. The jacket is really $300."*

If you're like most people, you're much more likely to buy the jacket in the first scenario. But that doesn't really make sense, does it? After all, the price you'd have to pay is exactly the same in both scenarios. So why are we more comfortable buying the jacket in the first one?

The answer is what psychologists refer to as anchoring.[22] As soon as we've read the price tag, we'll use it as a reference point—an anchor—for everything that happens after that.

If the initial price was higher, we'll feel like we're getting a good deal. And if the initial price was lower, we'll feel like we're getting a bad deal.

Marketers are well aware of this bias and use it to their advantage all the time. Here are some examples of anchoring strategies often used in marketing:

- Original vs discounted price—Retailers often present the old price of a product next to the new, discounted price. This way, the old price acts as an anchor that makes the new price more appealing.

- Price perception manipulation—Car dealerships often place their most expensive cars at the front of their display rooms. Once you've walked past them, the cars in the back don't seem all that expensive.

- Purchase quantity limits—Stores sometimes use signs like "Limit: 12 per customer." The number 12 then acts as an anchor that makes customers buy more than they intended.

And anchoring doesn't just occur in purchasing decisions. There are many examples of anchoring in everyday life, such as:

- Teacher's judgments—In some schools, children are tracked and categorized by ability from an early age. Those categories then become anchors that shape the teacher's expectations for the children.

- Longevity assumptions—If your parents lived to be very old, you'll likely expect to live a long life, too. But if your parents died young, you'll probably be surprised if you live for a long time.

- First impressions—When you meet someone for the first time, that encounter becomes a reference point for all future interactions. It's unfortunate and unfair, but first impressions matter A LOT.

As you can see, the anchoring bias has a huge impact on our lives. As you draw conclusions, form judgments, and make decisions, keep this sneaky tendency in mind.

Ask yourself if you are giving adequate consideration to all the information available, or if you're giving undue weight to some prior reference point. That way, you'll avoid getting stuck to irrelevant and irrational anchors.

8. HYPERBOLIC DISCOUNTING

*Our tendency to value smaller immediate
rewards more than larger future rewards.*

If you're like most people, you know very well what it's like to pro-crastinate. On more than one occasion, you've probably told yourself stuff like:

- "I should stick to my diet, but if I have a cupcake now, I can make up for it tomorrow."

- "I should go to the gym, but I really don't feel like it right now, so I'll get started Monday morning."

- "I should save more for retirement, but I want to buy a new phone, so I'll start saving next month."

Whenever you reason along these lines, you're falling victim to what behavioral economists call hyperbolic discounting.[23] It sounds complicated, but it just means that we value rewards differently at different points in time. In the short term, we're impatient and prefer immediate, smaller rewards. But in the long term, we're patient and prefer distant, bigger rewards.

A classic experiment[24] illustrates it well. When researchers offer people $100 today or $120 in a month, most people choose the $100. But if they offer people $100 in a year or $120 in a year and a month, suddenly, most people will wait the extra month to get the $120.

Even though the time and value difference are the exact same in both scenarios, we perceive them very differently. The further into the future a reward is, the more we tend to discount its value. So it's really no surprise that we consistently find ourselves procrastinating.

The short-term pleasures of eating a cupcake, taking a nap, or playing around with a new phone are immediate and tangible. Conversely, the long-term benefits of eating healthy, exercising, and saving money for retirement are far away and abstract.

That imbalance makes us choose short-term pleasures now while postponing long-term benefits for the future. A study on grocery-buying habits[25] demonstrates it nicely: when buying groceries online for delivery tomorrow, people buy a lot more ice cream and a lot fewer vegetables than when they're ordering for delivery next week.

The opposite of hyperbolic discounting is what psychologists call delayed gratification, the ability to resist smaller immediate rewards to receive larger future rewards.

Research links this ability with a host of positive life outcomes such as better grades, lower substance abuse rates, greater financial security, and improved physical and mental health.[26]

And it makes sense, doesn't it? No matter what goal you want to achieve, it almost always requires you to resist something easy and do something hard.

To be successful, you have to mitigate hyperbolic discounting so you can make wise choices in the moment and get better outcomes in the future.

We'll cover many ways to do that later on in this book but, for now, pay attention to effects that hyperbolic discounting is having on daily decision-making.

Consciously evaluate the tradeoff that you're making between the present and future, and try to make the best decision possible—even if it's uncomfortable.

If you regularly delay gratification, you'll become increasingly better at it. And your future self will be grateful for it.

9. DUNNING-KRUGER EFFECT

Our tendency to be more confident the less we know.

In 2005, I tried online poker for the first time. I learned the rules, deposited $30, and quickly doubled my money. There was no question in my mind—I was a natural at the game. So, I played again the next day… and quickly lost it all.

It wasn't until I started studying poker theory and strategy that I began to grasp the complexity of the game. I learned about pot odds, expected value, hand ranges, and many other concepts that I previously had been oblivious to.

The more I learned, the more I realized that I didn't understand. But my game kept improving. Eventually, I reached the point where I could play poker full time. And during those years, I noticed something interesting.

Beginners usually make every play with certainty, while experienced players question every decision. Bad players are confident, and good players doubtful. And that tendency doesn't just show up in poker but in any area of expertise.

In fact, it's so common that Bertrand Russell once stated, "The whole problem with the world is that fools and fanatics are always so certain of themselves, and wiser people so full of doubts."

And he's not alone; Socrates, William Shakespeare, Charles Darwin, and Friedrich Nietzsche have all commented on our propensity to be more confident the less we know.

But it wasn't until the late 1990s that this tendency was given a name. That's when social psychologists David Dunning and Justin Kruger did an experiment where they tested people's abilities in logical thinking, grammar, and sense of humor.

It turned out that those who performed the worst dramatically over-estimated their ability. And conversely, those who performed the best believed that they had in fact done poorly.

Dunning and Kruger reported their findings in an article called "Unskilled and unaware of it: how difficulties in recognizing one's own incompetence lead to inflated self-assessments,"[27] and the tendency came to be called the Dunning-Kruger effect.

According to David Dunning, "If you're incompetent, you can't know you're incompetent,"[28] and that has two major implications:

1) It leads to mistakes and poor decisions.
2) It prevents you from catching your errors.

In other words, not only does the Dunning-Kruger effect make you perform poorly, but it also makes it hard to recognize how badly you are in fact doing.

So, whenever you feel confident in a certain area of expertise, keep this tendency in mind. Remember that confidence might very well be a sign of invisible holes in your competence.

Be skeptical of your abilities, especially when you're a beginner. You'll make fewer mistakes, reach better decisions, and learn more from feedback.

10. BIAS BLIND SPOT

Our tendency to recognize biases in others
but fail to see them in ourselves.

As you learn about the cognitive biases in this book, you'll probably notice that they show up frequently in everyday life:

- Maybe you're discussing politics with a friend, and you spot a strong confirmation bias in his views.

- Perhaps someone expresses worry for a terrorist attack, and you realize it's because of availability bias from watching the news.

- Someone might tell you about the great deal they got on their new TV, and you recognize that they've fallen for the anchoring bias.

It's certainly useful to be aware of the mental errors going on around you. But the real benefit lies in identifying these flaws in your own thinking. It's only when you recognize the limitations of your cognitive apparatus that you can improve it.

Unfortunately, it's much harder to spot biases in ourselves than in others. In fact, that tendency is itself a mental error known as the bias blind spot or the bias bias. Behavioral decision researcher Erin McCormick provides this explanation.[29]

"When physicians receive gifts from pharmaceutical companies, they may claim that the gifts do not affect their decisions about what medicine to prescribe because they have no memory of the gifts biasing their prescriptions. However, if you ask them whether a gift might unconsciously bias the decisions of other physicians, most will agree that other physicians are unconsciously biased by the gifts, while continuing to believe that their own decisions are not. This disparity is the bias blind spot, and occurs for everyone, for many different types of judgments and decisions."

What's particularly striking about this tendency is how widespread it is. A study by McCormick and her colleagues[30] found that out of 661 participants, only one claimed to be more biased than the average person. The other 99.8 percent rated themselves as less biased than other people. And that, of course, is statistically impossible.

So why do we assume that we are less biased than others? A lot of it ties back into the self-serving bias, illusory superiority, and our tendency to protect our self-esteem. We generally consider biases undesirable, so we like to think of ourselves as unbiased or, at least, less biased than average.

But there's nothing wrong with being biased. As we've learned earlier in this book, biases are hardwired into our brains because we need them to navigate the world. And denying their influence only gets you stuck in your old ways of thinking.

So if you're still thinking that you're probably less biased than others, remember where that thought comes from. That's right—it comes from your brain. And your brain is biased to think that it's not biased.

Let go of the intuition that your thinking is somehow immune. Accept that you are just as vulnerable to thinking errors as everyone else. It's counterintuitive, but it will open you up for sharper judgment, smarter decisions, and better results.

PART 3: LOGICAL FALLACIES

It has been said that man is a rational animal. All my life I have been searching for evidence which could support this.

—Bertrand Russell

The Reasoning Flaws That Derail Your Judgment

Aristotle once described humans as "the rational animal." He claimed that rationality is our "distinguishing characteristic," the ability that sets us apart from all other animals.

Unlike other creatures, humans have the capacity to apply logic, establish facts, and make sense of things.

We do that by *reason*, and the process of doing so is called *reasoning*.

But just because we're capable of these things doesn't mean we're good at them.

Logical Fallacies

As we've seen in part 1 of the book, the brain is susceptible to cognitive biases—thinking errors in the way we process information.

On top of that, the brain doesn't appear to have evolved for precise logic. There are many reasoning traps that our minds fall into. These are called logical fallacies: "the modes in which, by neglecting the rules of logic, we often fall into erroneous reasoning."[31] Or, put simply: errors in reasoning.

Logical fallacies are like tricks or illusions of thought and, as such, they can often be difficult to spot. Let's, once again, use the organ donor study[32] as an example.

Swedish Organ Donors

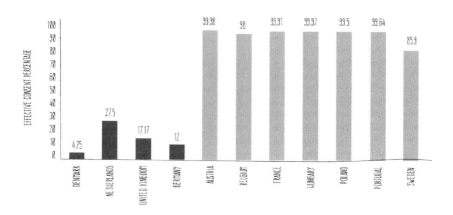

EFFECTIVE CONSENT RATES, BY COUNTRY. EXPLICIT CONSENT (OPT-IN, GOLD) AND PRESUMED CONSENT (OPT-OUT, BLUE)

Remember, this graph shows the percentage of people across several European countries who are willing to donate their organs after they die. This time note that Sweden, for whatever reason, has a slightly lower consent rate than the other countries on the right.

And now, let's imagine that you're in charge of increasing that number. How would you go about that?

One thing you could do is include a note on the organ donor form that says something like, "The vast majority of Swedes donate their organs."

That's a very persuasive statement that would probably convince a lot more people to donate. But, looking at it logically, it really shouldn't.

"Everybody's Doing It"

Donating your organs might very well be the right thing to do. But the fact that many people donate has nothing to do with it.

Just because something is popular, that doesn't make it the right decision. As we all know, a lot of people have been wrong about a lot of stuff a lot of times.

So if someone reads that "the vast majority of Swedes donate their organs" and chooses to donate based solely on that fact, they've fallen for a logical fallacy known as appeal to popularity.

And that's completely understandable. If something is popular, our common sense tells us it must also be good, true, or valid.

But that's not the case, and if we don't pay attention to logical pitfalls like this, they will cloud our judgment and create poor decisions.

Don't Be Fooled

By becoming aware of logical fallacies, you can identify and call out poor reasoning. You'll be able to examine information critically and adjust your decisions accordingly.

And that's an important skill, especially in a society where politicians, media, and marketers prey on logical fallacies to influence your decisions.

In the chapters ahead, we'll look at the most common logical fallacies relating to decision-making and how you can expose and prevent them.

And we'll begin with one I'm sure you've come across many times…

1. HASTY GENERALIZATION

Our tendency to draw conclusions based on small sample sizes.

Imagine I told you that the average height of all the people in the entire world is about 6.2 feet. And when you ask me how I learned that, I replied, "It was simple, really. I just measured myself."

After getting over the initial shock of my apparent stupidity, you'd probably inform me that I can't just measure myself and draw such a conclusion. I'd need a much larger sample size.

And, of course, you'd be right. In obvious examples like this, we have an intuitive sense for what statisticians call the law of large numbers,[33] which states, "As a sample size grows, its mean gets closer to the average of the whole population."

But there are many less clear-cut situations where we fail to take sample size into account. Consider, for example, this statement:

In a telephone poll of 300 seniors, 60 percent support the president.[34]

If you had to create a headline of three words to describe those findings, what would it be? If you're like most people, you'll write "Elderly Support President."

And those words do a good job of conveying the essence of the story. But the details of the poll design—that it was done over the phone with a sample of just 300—gets left out.

The takeaway? We pay much more attention to the *content* of messages than we do to the *reliability* of the information.

You've probably seen plenty of commercials where four out of five dentists recommend some toothpaste. That seems convincing, but only because we focus on the *content* of the message—authorities in the field think highly of the product.

If we instead turned our attention to the *reliability* of the information—the fact that we don't know the sample size—we'd come to a very different conclusion. After all, there's a good chance only five dentists were actually asked. And if you did a proper poll with a random sampling of 1000 dentists, perhaps only 20 percent would recommend the brand.

Accurate assumptions require sufficient sample sizes. But in everyday life, we often forget about that and, as a result, make hasty generalizations. Here are a few examples:

- Your dad smokes four packs of cigarettes per day and lives to be eighty years old. He's just one person, but you still conclude that smoking can't be that bad for you.

- You meet someone for the first time, and he makes a bad impression on you. It's just one meeting, but you still assume that he's a rude person.

- You try investing in the stock market and lose half of the money spent in your first week. It's a short period of time, but you still conclude the stock market isn't for you.

As you can see, hasty generalizations often lead to inaccurate conclusions, bad judgments, and poor decisions. So always pay attention to the reliability of information. When the sample size is small, suspend your judgment and try to find more reliable data.

2. FALSE CAUSE

Our tendency to presume that one thing caused another.

Imagine that it's a sunny day at the beach. It's terribly hot, so you decide to cool off in the ocean. As you make your way to the shoreline, you spot an ice cream stand.

Before you decide whether or not to treat yourself, consider the following statistical fact: when sales of ice cream go up, so do deaths by drowning. How should that information affect your decision?

If you're like most people, you'll assume that having ice cream before going into the water is dangerous. But it's really not, and to understand why, we need to recognize the difference between correlation and causation.

Correlation means that there is a relationship between two things. Causation means that one thing causes another thing to happen.

A correlation between two things doesn't necessarily mean there is causation between the two. So the fact that there is a relationship between ice cream sales and deaths by drowning doesn't mean that ice cream causes drowning.

Instead, the correlation depends on a third factor: temperature. When it's hot outside, people buy more ice cream. They're also more likely to go swimming, which increases the number of drownings. So, ice cream sales and deaths by drowning correlate with each other—but only because they both correlate with temperature.

Whenever there's a relationship between two things, we tend to assume that one of them caused the other. But as any good statistician will tell you, correlation does not equal causation.[35] And there are plenty of quite funny statistical findings that illustrate this.[36] For example, during the years of 2000 through 2009:

- The number of people who drowned by falling into a swimming pool correlates with the number of films Nicolas Cage appeared in.

- The per capita cheese consumption correlates with the number of people who died by becoming tangled in their bedsheets.

- The divorce rate in Maine, New England, correlates with the per capita margarine consumption.

How can these things correlate? Well, if you have a big enough pile of data, you can find plenty of variables that just happen to have a statistical correlation.

It's a complete coincidence, but still, it's very tempting to try to come up with an explanation for why Nicolas Cage's movies makes people stumble into pools. It's human nature to force causal links:

- "My friend ignores me because she's mad at me."

- "I failed the test because I suck at math."

- "The team is failing because of the coach."

Explanations like these help us bind facts together, but they're often inaccurate. The world is a complicated place, and we overestimate our ability to understand the connections within it.

Maybe your friend is just having a bad day. Perhaps you failed the test because you've never had a decent math teacher. And the team might be failing because the players aren't putting in the necessary work.

These things are very hard to know for sure, so pay attention to your tendency to presume that one thing caused another. Be skeptical of your assumptions, open to alternative explanations, and willing to change your mind. That way, you'll be less vulnerable to false cause reasoning.

3. FALSE DILEMMA

Our tendency to consider only two options even though more exist.

In a 2011 TV commercial,[37] the moving company United Van Lines asked:

"Is United right for your move? Ask yourself, do you want:

- (A) A seamless professional move? or (B) Your possessions set on fire?

- (A) Technology experts to set up your home network? or (B) Raccoons to run amok with your electronics?

- (A) Portable containers to move yourself? or (B) Complete chaos?

If you answered A, call United."

Now, if you're like me, you're not thrilled about the prospect of chaos. You don't want raccoons to fiddle with your electronics. And you certainly don't want to see all your stuff go up in flames.

But does that mean you have to call United the next time you move? The answer, of course, is no. And the reason for that is that their commercial (although admittedly funny) sets up a false dilemma.

This is a fallacy that occurs when only two options are presented even though, in reality, more choices exist. False dilemmas are usually presented as "either this or that" statements, but they can also come in the form of left-out options.

Sometimes they arise unintentionally, but they can also be used as a rhetorical strategy. When used deliberately, the persuader presents an unacceptable option as the only alternative to the one they want you to choose. Here are some examples:

- "Either we increase taxes, or we learn to live with crumbling roads." (There are many other ways to fund infrastructure.)

- "You are either with us or against us." (You can be on neither side.)

- "America: Love it or leave it." (You can enjoy some parts, be critical of others, and still be a citizen.)

- "I thought you were a good person, but you weren't at church today." (Many good people don't attend church.)

- "Either you buy me this book, or you don't think it's important that I learn to read." (You can refuse to buy the book and still value your daughter's education.)

Other varieties include false trilemmas, which is when three options are presented, false quadrilemmas, which is when four options are presented, and so on. Any time certain options are considered the only possibilities when more exist, it's a logical fallacy.

And whether or not it's brought on intentionally, this reasoning flaw can trick you into making choices you wouldn't have made if you had considered all the options available.

So when you're presented with "either this or that" type statements or a limited number of choices, pause and reflect. Ask yourself if the options are truly mutually exclusive and if they are really the only choices available. That will open up your mind to more possibilities and better decisions.

4. MINDLE GROUND

Our tendency to assume that the middle point
between two extremes must be true.

In the last chapter we covered the false dilemma fallacy, our tendency to consider only two options even though more exist. The middle ground fallacy is effectively an inverse false dilemma. That is, instead of only considering two options, we only focus on a middle point between them.

Let's say James is convinced that vaccinations causes autism in children. But his friend John, who's a doctor, says that claim has been debunked and proven false. Listening to their discussion, their mutual friend Robert concludes that vaccinations must cause autism sometimes, but not all the time.

While the correct position on a topic often is somewhere between two extremes, that cannot be assumed without considering the evidence.

Sometimes, one of the extreme positions is entirely true, and the other one completely false. When that's the case, a compromise always misses the mark.

Other times, both extreme positions are wrong. And when that's the case, the truth can't be found anywhere in the spectrum between them.

If we don't pay attention to it, the middle ground fallacy can lead to poor reasoning and bad decisions. Let's have a look at some more examples:

- My teacher says it's never okay to skip classes. My friend Michael says it's okay to skip as many classes as you want. Therefore, it's okay to skip class sometimes.

- Jennifer thinks I should follow my doctor's prescription to treat my illness. Linda says I should use holistic medicine. Therefore, I'll take half of my prescriptions and half of the recommendations from holistic medicine.

- William thinks the Philadelphia Eagles will win the game. David thinks the New England Patriots will win. Therefore, I'll place a large bet that the game ends in a tie.

- Some people believe in man-made climate change. Others claim global warming isn't real. Therefore, climate change is real, but people aren't causing it.

- Some people think slavery is wrong. Other people think slavery is right. Therefore, we should allow slavery in some places but not all.

Compromises are often useful, but not always. As the saying goes, half a kitten is not half as cute, it's a bloody mess.

Whenever you're presented with two opposing views, don't automatically assume that the truth has to exist somewhere between them.

Instead, examine the evidence of each claim independently. Ask yourself how likely they are to be true, and if a compromise between them is truly warranted. That will help you make more accurate assumptions and better choices.

5. SLIPPERY SLOPE

*Our tendency to assume that a minor action
will lead to a major consequence.*

High school student David wants to spend the weekend with his friends, but his mom won't let him. *"You have to study on Saturdays,"* she insists. *"If you don't, your grades will suffer, you won't get into a good university, and you'll end up flipping burgers for the rest of your life!"*

This is a prime example of the slippery slope fallacy: assuming that a relatively small first step will lead to a chain of events that eventually culminates in a significant, usually negative, outcome.

In other words, you assume that if A occurs, then B will follow, and if B occurs, then C will follow. And since C is something you really don't want, you shouldn't allow A to happen.

Some slippery slopes are real, but often they're not, and that's when we've got a slippery slope fallacy on our hands. To analyze this kind of reasoning, we need to examine each link in the chain.

Let's assign some rough probability estimates to every assumption David's mom is making. She's saying that, if he doesn't study on Saturdays:

A: *"Your grades will suffer."* It's possible but not very likely. A lot of students get good grades without studying on weekends. Let's give this a 5 percent probability estimate.

B: *"You won't get into a good university."* That depends on what counts as a good university. David could also be eligible for non-academic scholarships. We'll give this a probability of, say, 10 percent.

C: *"You'll end up flipping burgers for the rest of your life."* This is obviously the weakest link in the chain. It's really nothing but wildly pessimistic speculation. It gets a probability of 0.1 percent.

As you can see, every link in the chain is weak. And the chain as a whole compounds those weaknesses. Here's how the math works out:

.05 x .10 x .001 = There's a 0.0005 percent risk that David's mom's assumption is correct. Not a very slippery slope.

Of course, it's very difficult to predict the likelihood of a complex chain reaction. We can't know if our probability numbers are accurate. But a rough guesstimate can still provide a useful hint about the likelihood of a chain of events.

So when you come across slippery slope assumptions, tease out the links in the chain and ask yourself how likely each of them is to be true. Then keep these two things in mind:

1) The chain is only as strong as its weakest link. If you spot just one weak claim, the entire line of reasoning is also weak.

2) Weaknesses in the links have a compounding effect. The strength of the whole chain is almost always even weaker than its weakest link.

Be skeptical of hypothetical chain reactions, and you'll be much less vulnerable to falling for slippery slope reasoning.

6. SUNK COST FALLACY

*Our tendency to do things based on how much
time and resources we've invested.*

Imagine that you go to see a movie. You pay for a ticket and take your seat. But about 30 minutes in, you realize that the movie you're watching is terrible. What should you do?

If you're like most people, you'll finish the movie anyway. You've paid for it, after all, and you want to get your money's worth.

But that decision is actually irrational. Why? Because the ticket purchase is a "sunk cost"; it's money already spent that cannot be recovered.

And, as economists will tell you, sunk costs are not taken into account when making rational decisions.

How so? Well, in the movie scenario, you have two choices:

1) Pay the price of the ticket and waste the time it takes to finish it.

2) Pay the price of the ticket and not waste the time it takes to finish it.

Since the second option only involves one loss (money spent), while the first involves two losses (money spent and time wasted), an economist would say that the second option is obviously preferable.

You've already paid for the ticket, so that part of the decision no longer affects the future. Therefore, the current choice should be based solely on whether you want to see the movie at all, regardless of the price, just as if it were free.

Now, of course, that's easier said than done. In reality, we often fall for the "sunk cost fallacy" and routinely let our current actions be affected by the money, time, and effort we've previously invested into something.[38]

This tendency shows up all the time in small everyday decisions like:

- "I'm full, but I might as well keep eating because I've paid for the food."

- "This book is boring, but I've already read 100 pages so I might as well finish it."

- "I haven't used this sweater in years, but it was so expensive that I have to keep it."

And it can also affect big life decisions like:

- "I've invested so much into this business venture that I might as well keep pouring money into it."

- "This career isn't fulfilling to me, but I'll stick to it because I've invested so much time and money into my education."

- "I know my partner is bad for me, but we've been together for so long that it wouldn't make sense to leave."

As you can imagine, the sunk cost fallacy can have a considerable influence on our lives. So, when you make decisions, try to let bygones be bygones. Ignore costs from the past, base your decision solely on the present, and you'll be much better off in the future.

7. PLANNING FALLACY

Our tendency to underestimate the time and
resources needed to complete something.

Do you underestimate the time it will take you to get to work in the morning? Have you ever raced to meet a deadline? Do you struggle to keep your monthly budget?

If your answer to any of these questions is "Yes," then you know what's it's like to fall for the planning fallacy. And you're not alone. Research shows that we all tend to underestimate the time and resources needed to finish things.

A great illustration of this comes from a study in which students were asked to estimate when they would complete their personal academic projects.[39] The results showed that less than half of them finished by the time they were 99 percent sure they would be done. Even when they were asked to make "highly conservative forecasts," predictions the students were pretty much certain they would fulfill, their estimates were still way too optimistic.

And the planning fallacy doesn't just occur in individual tasks. It also affects group projects, which can magnify its consequences dramatically. Consider, for example, the following massive construction overruns:

- The Denver International Airport opened sixteen months later than scheduled with a total cost of $4.8 billion—over $2 billion more than expected.[40]
- The Eurofighter Typhoon, a joint defense project of several European countries, took six years longer and cost €8 billion more than initially planned.[41]

- The Sydney Opera House, originally estimated to be finished in 1963 for $7 million, was completed ten years later for a grand total of $102 million.[42]

I know, crazy, right? Why are we so terrible at estimating the time and resources needed to finish projects? A clue to the underlying problem comes from a study[43] where the researchers found that asking people for their predictions based on realistic "best guess" scenarios, versus hoped-for "best case" scenarios, produced indistinguishable results.

It turns out that when we're asked for a "best guess" scenario, we envision that everything will go exactly as planned. As a result, we end up with a vision that is exactly the same as our "best case." And since reality is full of unforeseen delays, this way of thinking creates a lot of problems, delays, and stress.

A much more useful approach is what researchers call "reference class forecasting": predicting the future by looking at similar past situations and their outcomes. In other words, instead of guessing, you base your plans on available data.

- When planning how much time you need to get ready in the morning, don't imagine what tomorrow morning will be like. Consider how much time you usually need every morning and use that as your estimate.

- When scheduling a project at work, don't guess how long it will take you to complete. Find out how long this kind of project typically takes and plan accordingly.

- When creating your monthly budget, don't just write down what you would ideally like to spend. Look at what you're typically spending each month and start from there.

Planning this way will give you an accurate understanding of the time and resources needed. That will make your plans realistic and useful. As a result, you'll be remarkably productive and efficient.

8. APPEAL TO POPULARITY

Our tendency to believe something is true just because it's popular.

Let's begin this chapter with a quick trip down memory lane. When you were a kid, did you ever try to convince your parents to buy you a Pet Rock, Transformer, Furby, or whatever the popular fad toy of your childhood was?

Stating your case, you probably said something like, "Everyone at school has one! And they say it's the best toy ever, so I have to have one, too!" To which, inevitably, your parents responded something like, "If everyone at school jumped off a cliff, would you do it, too?"

With that response, whether or not they knew it, your parents were pointing out a flaw in your reasoning known as "appeal to popularity." This is a fallacy that occurs when something is considered being good, true, or valid solely because it's popular.

The reasoning goes like this: "Everybody is doing X. Therefore, X must be the right thing to do." That kind of thinking is problematic because, as your parents pointed out, the majority isn't always right.

Something can be true, even if everyone believes it's false. And something can be false, even if everyone believes it's true.

When stated in such explicit language, few people think they'd fall for such stupid reasoning. But even among adults it's a remarkably common fallacy. The reason is that our intuition tells us that if an idea is popular, it must have some truth to it.

But ideas don't get popular because they're true. They get popular because they're, well, popular. This phenomenon is called the "bandwagon effect": if an idea gains some attraction, that will, in and of itself, attract more interest.

That interest then generates even more interest and, before you know it, everyone is jumping on the bandwagon and giving their support for the idea. It doesn't matter if the idea is true or not. The bandwagon has its own momentum and will carry its passengers either way.

Now, that doesn't mean that you should completely disregard popular ideas. Sometimes what the majority believes is actually true. For example, if most scientists accept that the universe is about 13.7 billion years old, it's wise to believe them because they can present good evidence for their claim.

But in most cases, it's important to treat appeals to popularity with a healthy dose of skepticism. If you don't, you handicap your judgment and risk making poor decisions. For example:

- *"This book doesn't look all that great, but it has sold a million copies, so I'll buy it."*

- *"It's against the law to lie on your taxes, but everyone does it, so I'll do it, too."*

- *"Everyone at work sleeps just five hours per night, so I'll start cutting back on my sleep."*

In the words of Mark Twain: *"Whenever you find yourself on the side of the majority, it is time to pause and reflect."* Deliberately choose the bandwagons you jump on, and you'll make wiser choices and get better results.

9. APPEAL TO AUTHORITY

Our tendency to believe something is true just because it's the opinion of an expert.

When people present an argument, they sometimes refer to the opinion of some authority as evidence for their claim. This is often a person, but it can also be something like a book, a website, or a constitution.

That kind of reasoning can be problematic, especially if the person insists their claim must be true merely because some authority said so. It is not that an expert says it that makes a claim true. What makes it true is the preponderance of evidence for their theory.

An argument from an authority can never prove that something is true. It can, however, make it more likely to be true. But that's only the case if the authority referred to is actually an expert on the topic at hand.

If the expert is relevant, an appeal to authority is sound. But if the expert is irrelevant, the argument is fallacious. When you come across this kind of reasoning, the trick is to evaluate the relevancy of the expert. Let's look at some examples:

> *"Mozart heavily influenced Beethoven. I know so because I looked it up online."*

This is an appeal to non-authority. It's fallacious because we know nothing about the reliability of the website. The internet as a whole can't be trusted as a reliable authority on anything.

> *"Eating cooked meat causes cancer. I know so because scientists say so."*

This is an appeal to anonymous authorities. It's fallacious since we don't know who these scientists are. If we're unfamiliar with the research, we can't know how reliable it is.

"God doesn't exist. I know so because Stephen Hawking said so."

This is an appeal to unqualified authority. It's fallacious because, while Stephen Hawking was a brilliant physicist, that doesn't automatically make him an authority on whether God exists.

"I need to take my medicine. I know so because my doctor prescribed it."

This is an appeal to legitimate authority. It's not fallacious, because the authority has expertise relevant to the claim. Assuming that the doctor has the right medical training, you can confidently follow the prescription.

Now, there's always a chance that even a highly relevant authority could be wrong, so it's always a good idea to think of facts as provisionally true. Accept information from credible experts as correct, but be willing to change your mind whenever you come across an argument with more trustworthy facts.

Question authority and analyze evidence. That way, you'll be more flexible in your beliefs and less vulnerable to irrelevant expert opinions.

10. THE FALLACY FALLACY

*Our tendency to assume that when a fallacy
is made, the claim must be wrong.*

As you learn about the logical fallacies in this book, you'll probably find plenty of examples in your everyday life.

- Maybe someone makes a bad first impression on you, and you conclude he's a rude person. But then you realize that's a hasty generalization. You can't draw that conclusion based on such a small sample size.

- Perhaps a friend tells you that she doesn't feel well because of the fish she ate yesterday. You identify this as a false cause fallacy. She can't know that it's necessarily the fish that caused her to feel bad.

- Someone might recommend a book, telling you that "everyone loves it." And you recognize this as an appeal to popularity. How popular the book is says little about whether you'll enjoy it.

And when you spot a fallacy, it's tempting to think that the claim must be wrong. But that assumption is actually itself a fallacy aptly named the fallacy fallacy. You see, it's entirely possible to reason poorly, use a variety of fallacies, and still arrive at a true conclusion.

- The person you met might actually be rude. You can't know it from just one meeting, but it's fully possible that future encounters will be equally unpleasant.

- Your friend does indeed feel bad because of the fish she had. There are many factors that could have caused it, but the fish might just be the correct one.

- The book someone recommended might just be spectacular. While the claim that "everyone loves it" isn't very useful, it could still turn out to be an excellent read.

The takeaway? A fallacy is never evidence against the claim. It's just evidence for poor reasoning.

Being able to identify logical fallacies is an important skill that can dramatically improve your thinking. But if you concentrate too much on them, you can lose sight of the content within the reasoning. And if you focus too much on calling them out, well, then you'll risk becoming an annoying know-it-all.

So whenever you spot a fallacy, keep this helpful command in mind:

> *"Don't shoot the message. Just because the messenger is stupid, doesn't mean the message is."*[44]

PART 4: MENTAL MODELS

Point of view is worth 80 IQ points.

—Alan Kay

THE THINKING TOOLS OF THE MIND

"Why did the chicken cross the road?"

According to biologist Robert Sapolsky, the answer to that question will depend on the expert you ask.[45] For example:

- A biologist might say: "The chicken crossed the road because it saw a potential mate on the other side."

- A kinesiologist might say: "The chicken crossed the road because the muscles in its legs contracted and pulled its leg bones forward."

- A neuroscientist might say: "The chicken crossed the road because the neurons in its brain fired and triggered it to move."

Interestingly, all of these experts are correct. But at the same time, none of them are seeing the entire picture. And that's because all of them are looking at the question through the lens of their unique expertise.

Mental Models

A mental model is a representation of how something works. It's a concept, framework, or worldview stored in your mind that you use to interpret, simplify, and understand the world. For example:

- Second-Level Thinking is a mental model that helps you identify subsequent consequences before they happen.

- Incentives is a mental model that helps you understand what motivates people.

- Entropy is a mental model that helps you understand how everything in life moves from order to disorder.

Mental models guide your perceptions, thoughts, and actions. They are the thinking tools your mind uses to explain reality, solve problems, and make decisions.

The Limitations of Expertise

The quality of your decisions depends on the mental models in your mind. If you have a lot of mental models—a big toolbox—you're better equipped to perceive reality accurately and find solutions to problems.

Most of us, however, don't have a big toolbox to pick and choose from. Instead, we default back to just a few tools again and again. Usually, these are mental models related to our discipline and expertise.

A biologist will tend to think in terms of evolution. A kinesiologist will tend to think in terms of mechanisms of movement. And a neuroscientist will tend to think in terms of the nervous system and the brain.

The more you master a particular mental model, the more you'll start applying it everywhere. You'll cram reality into your model of it. And so what looks like expertise can actually become a limitation.

As the proverb goes: "If all you have is a hammer, everything looks like a nail."

Expanding Your Toolbox

If your set of mental models is limited, so is your ability to find solutions. To make wise choices, you have to collect a wide range of mental models. In other words, you have to have a well-equipped decision-making toolbox.

The good news? Acquiring new thinking tools is straightforward. Once you learn a mental model, you can't unlearn it. And from that point forward, you can use it anytime you want to shift your perspective and find new solutions.

What's more, you don't have to master every idea from every discipline to become a great thinker. If you can just get a firm grasp of a few fundamental models, you'll develop a remarkably accurate and useful picture of reality.

In the chapters ahead, we'll cover the most widely applicable mental models for decision-making. And we'll begin with a very useful idea for understanding how the mind works.

1. SYSTEM 1 AND SYSTEM 2

The two modes of thought.

Imagine that I ask you, "What's 2 + 2?"

You can't help but think of the answer. The number "4" instantly pops into your head. If you've learned basic math, it's impossible not to immediately think of the answer. This is the result of what scientists call reflexive brain.

Now, imagine that I instead ask you, "What's 39 multiplied by 26?"

Most likely, your brain goes blank. It doesn't have an instant answer. Unless you're a math wizard, you have to go through the tedious process of calculating it. You have to use what is known as your reflective brain.

In his book *Thinking Fast and Slow*, Daniel Kahneman termed these two modes of thought as System 1 (reflexive) and System 2 (reflective):[46]

> *"System 1 operates automatically and quickly, with little or no effort and no sense of voluntary control. System 2 allocates attention to the effortful mental activities that demand it, including complex computations."*

In other words, System 1 is intuitive, and System 2 is deliberate. These two modes of thought complement each other, and they're both active whenever we're awake.

System 1 is the first layer of thinking that our brains delegate problems to. System 2 only comes into the picture when System 1 doesn't have an answer.

That arrangement usually works pretty well because System 1 is generally good at what it does. It's not perfect, however, and there are many situations where decisions should ideally be delegated to System 2, but System 1 makes them anyway.

As an example, consider the simple math problem below. Don't try to solve it—just observe the intuitive answer that comes to mind:

The total cost of a baseball bat and ball is $1.10. The cost of the bat is $1.00 more than the ball. How much does the ball cost?

System 1 will tell you that the ball costs 10 cents, which is the wrong answer. If you do the math using System 2, you'll realize that the right answer is 5 cents (and $1.05 for the bat).

This example illustrates the problem with System 1. While fast and effortless, it's also prone to mistakes. In fact, the sloppiness of System 1 is what creates the cognitive biases and logical fallacies we covered previously in the book.

But despite its flaws, you shouldn't try to turn off System 1 and operate solely in System 2. According to Kahneman, that wouldn't be possible nor desirable:[47]

> *"Constantly questioning our own thinking would be impossibly tedious, and System 2 is much too slow and inefficient to serve as a substitute for System 1 in making routine decisions. The best we can do is a compromise: learn to recognize situations in which mistakes are likely and try harder to avoid significant mistakes when the stakes are high."*

When you're making mundane and inconsequential decisions, let System 1 run. It's okay that it's wrong now and again because it saves valuable mental energy and reduces decision fatigue.

But when you're about to make an important decision, switch to System 2. Deliberately slow down, take your time, and use the mental models in the chapters ahead to reach the best decision possible.

2. THE MAP IS NOT THE TERRITORY

An abstraction derived from something is not the thing itself.

In 1931, mathematician Alfred Korzybski presented a paper in which he introduced the idea that the map is not the territory.[48] A map always comes with certain inherent problems. Here are some of its limitations:

- A map can be wrong without you realizing it.

- A map is by definition a reduction of the territory, which means it leaves out certain important information.

- A map needs interpretation, which is a process that often leads to mistakes.

- A map can be outdated and represent something that has changed or no longer exists.

The distinction between map and territory is a useful metaphor of the differences between impression and reality. What you think something is like differs from what it's really like.

Imagine, for example, that you're checking out the social media profile of an acquaintance. Browsing through her countless updates of happy pictures, you conclude that she has to be a happy person. But the map is not the territory. The life she's portraying on social media says little about what her life is really like.

And there are many other examples of where we confuse the map with the territory. A commercial is not the product. An online dating profile is not the person. A documentary is not the complete picture. A resume is not the applicant. A test score is not your intelligence.

On a deeper level, your perceptions of reality can also be considered maps. Your brain takes what you perceive through your senses and creates maps of reality written in neural patterns. And that kind of map is just as problematic as any other.

Why? Well, firstly, our senses are neurologically limited and only operate within a certain bandwidth. Our brains are not equipped to perceive the full range of reality. Which is why, for example, we can't hear the ultrasonic sounds of a bat.

Secondly, as we've seen in previous chapters, our minds are heavily influenced by cognitive biases that distort our thinking and logical fallacies that derail our reasoning. Which is why, for example, we unduly favor information that confirms our existing beliefs.

So as we create our inner representations of the external world, we do so using incomplete and distorted information. As a result, we often end up with beliefs that don't match up with reality.

A map is never the same as the territory, and most of us struggle to make that distinction. In the words of author Shane Parrish:

> *"For many people, the model creates its own reality. It is as if the spreadsheet comes to life. We forget that reality is a lot messier. The map isn't the territory. The theory isn't what it describes, it's simply a way we choose to interpret a certain set of information. Maps can also be wrong, but even if they are essentially correct, they are an abstraction, and abstraction means that information is lost to save space."*[49]

Be skeptical of maps. Remember their limitations. And always be willing to switch them out whenever you find a better one. That way, you'll be less rigid in your thinking and more accurate in your judgments. And that's a great foundation for making intelligent decisions.

3. THE 80/20 PRINCIPLE

80 percent of the effects come from 20 percent of the causes.

In the late 1800s, Italian economist Vilfredo Pareto was tending his garden when he made a small discovery that would have huge implications.

He noticed that a minority of the pea pods in his garden produced a majority of the peas. And that got him thinking about economic output on a larger scale. Could this unequal distribution be taking place in other areas as well?

At the time, Pareto was studying the wealth of different nations. As he started analyzing the distribution of wealth in his home country, he indeed found that about 80 percent of the land in Italy was owned by just 20 percent of the population. Expanding his work into other countries, Pareto found that a similar distribution applied in those places, too.[50]

Similar to the pea pods in his garden, the majority of resources were controlled by a minority of the group. And as he continued his research in various societies, industries, and even companies, this trend turned out to be remarkably consistent. The numbers were never quite the same, but the approximate 4-to-1 ratio kept showing up.

Over time, this idea—that a minority of things account for the majority of results—became known as the Pareto Principle or, as it's commonly referred to these days, the 80/20 principle.[51]

Since Pareto's discovery, the 80/20 principle has been most popular in business settings. Companies have often found that, for example:

- 20 percent of their customers brought in 80 percent of their revenue.
- 20 percent of their sales reps closed 80 percent of their sales.
- 20 percent of their costs made up 80 percent of their total expenses.

And that's valuable information that can help increase efficiency and profits for companies. But the 80/20 principle is just as useful outside of business. You can ask yourself, for instance:

- Which 20 percent of your relationships create 80 percent of your happiness?
- What 20 percent of your daily habits account for 80 percent of your well-being?
- What 20 percent of your stuff do you use 80 percent of the time?

By answering questions like these, you can increase the efficiencies in your life. You'll know who to spend your time with, what daily habits to focus on, and what clothes to keep in your closet.

And those are just a few examples, of course. The 80/20 principle is very useful anytime you want to figure out the most impactful causes and efficient actions.

In fact, it's a great way to consume this book. As you keep reading, think about which 20 percent of the chapters will provide 80 percent of usefulness to you. Then focus on learning those ideas first.

Get into the habit of thinking 80/20, and you'll spend a lot more time on what's truly essential.

4. THE CIRCLE OF COMPETENCE

The subject area that matches a person's skills or expertise.

In his 1996 shareholder letter,[52] legendary investor Warren Buffett wrote:

> *"What an investor needs is the ability to correctly evaluate selected businesses. Note that word "selected": You don't have to be an expert on every company, or even many. You only have to be able to evaluate companies within your circle of competence. The size of that circle is not very important; knowing its boundaries, however, is vital."*

Everyone builds up knowledge on certain areas throughout their lives. Some areas are widely understood, while others require more specific expertise.

For example, most of us have a basic understanding of the economics of a restaurant. You buy or rent a place, furnish it, and hire employees to cook, serve, and clean.

From there, it's all about setting the right prices and generating enough traffic to make a profit on what you serve after your expenses have been paid.

The menu, atmosphere, and pricing will vary, but all restaurants follow the same economic formula. That basic knowledge, combined with some understanding of accounting and a little bit of study, is enough to allow you to evaluate and invest in restaurants. It's not too complicated.

However, most of us don't have the same understanding of how a biotech drug company works. And, according to Buffett, that's perfectly fine. To be a successful investor, you don't have to understand every business you come across. But you have to understand what you know—your circle of competence—and stick to those areas.

Buffett's business partner Charlie Munger applies this idea to life in general:[53]

> *"You have to figure out what your own aptitudes are. If you play games where other people have the aptitudes and you don't, you're going to lose. And that's as close to certain as any prediction that you can make. You have to figure out where you've got an edge. And you've got to play within your own circle of competence."*

To give you a concrete example, I'll share my circle of competence. It contains three major areas:

1) Writing. This is the number one keystone habit of my business. So before I do anything else each day, I write for at least two hours.

2) Learning. To be a good writer, I need a lot of good ideas to write about. So I spend time every day educating myself on things my readers want to learn about.

3) Marketing. I want to reach and serve as many people as possible. To do that, I spend a lot of time learning about stuff like online marketing, persuasion, consumer psychology, and so on.

Each workday that I learn something, write something, and promote what I wrote, I consider a day well spent. Conversely, each workday I stray outside of these three areas, I generally see as a day poorly spent.

That's the power of a well-defined circle of competence. It makes you a lot less vulnerable to the Dunning-Kruger effect. You'll be acutely aware of what you know and what you don't know. And that helps you spend your time, energy, and resources much more efficiently.

What's your circle of competence? Do you know its boundaries? And are you operating inside of it?

5. OPPORTUNITY COST

The benefits missed when choosing one option over another.

Imagine a stove with four burners on it that each represents a major area of your life:

- The first burner is your family.

- The second burner is your friends.

- The third burner is your health.

- The fourth burner is your work.

The Four Burners Theory says, "In order to be successful, you have to cut off one of your burners. And in order to be really successful, you have to cut off two."[54]

If you want a successful career and a happy marriage, then you won't have as much time for working out and seeing your friends. If you want to be healthy and succeed as a parent, then you won't have as much time to put into your career.

Of course, you can choose to spend your time equally among all four burners, but then you'll never achieve your full potential in any of the areas.

It's quite a predicament, and there's no perfect solution for it. But the Four Burners Theory is still useful because it highlights an important fact of life that we tend to overlook:

Making decisions requires trading off one goal against another.[55]

We continuously face decisions between the benefits and costs of one option and the benefits and costs of another option. The problem is that the benefits are usually much more readily apparent than the costs.

And that's why it's important to understand the concept economists call opportunity cost: "the loss of potential gain from other alternatives when one alternative is chosen."

You can think of it this way: Every time you say yes to something, you're also saying no to something else. The thing you say no to would have given you certain benefits. And now that you're not getting them, they are your opportunity costs.

Imagine, for example, that you're browsing Amazon looking for a book to read. When you find an interesting title, all the possible benefits are readily available on the book page. But what is less obvious is the opportunity cost of the book. That is, the benefits from the other books you could read instead.

Considering opportunity costs in your decisions is important because it helps you to assess different courses of action more accurately. Before I knew about it, I jumped on a lot of exciting business opportunities that came my way because I focused solely on the benefits.

But I've since learned that each of these endeavors comes with a steep opportunity cost. Every time I say yes to some appealing new opportunity, I also say no to researching, writing, and marketing my books. Sure, I might gain some nice short-term benefits, but they're rarely worth straying outside my circle of competence and losing momentum in my author career.

How about you? In what areas of your life do you need to start considering the opportunity costs? And what changes do you need to make to get the greatest return on your limited time, energy, and money?

6. THE EISENHOWER MATRIX

Prioritizing what's important over what's urgent.

Dwight D. Eisenhower lived a remarkably productive life.

From 1953 to 1961, he served two terms as President of the United States. During that time, he initiated several programs that directly led to, among many other things, the development of the Interstate Highway System, the launch of the internet, and the establishment of NASA.

Before his time in office, he was a five-star general in the United States Army. Serving as Supreme Allied Commander in Europe during the Second World War, he was responsible for planning and executing invasions of Germany, France, and North Africa.

At other points during his career, Eisenhower also served as president of Columbia University as well as the first ever Supreme Commander of NATO. And, as if all that wasn't enough, he also somehow made time for hobbies like golfing, cooking, and oil painting.

Considering his incredible ability to get things done, it's no surprise that his time management methods are still being taught to this day. His most famous productivity strategy is called the Eisenhower Matrix,[56] and it's a very useful model for prioritizing your tasks. To use it, you sort your tasks into four categories depending on their importance and urgency:

1) Important and urgent–Tasks you will do immediately.

2) Important but not urgent–Tasks you will schedule for later.

3) Not important but urgent–Tasks you will delegate.

4) Not important nor urgent–Tasks you will eliminate.

The key here is to distinguish between important and urgent tasks. So what's the difference? *Important* tasks are things that contribute to your long-term goals. *Urgent* tasks are things that require immediate attention. To give you an example of what an Eisenhower Matrix might look like, here's mine for today:

	URGENT	NOT URGENT
IMPORTANT	**IMPORTANT AND URGENT** • WRITING THE CHAPTER ON THE EISENHOWER MATRIX.	**IMPORTANT, BUT NOT URGENT** • RESEARCHING UPCOMING CHAPTERS. • REVIEWING MY BOOK MARKETING CAMPAIGN. • GOING TO THE GYM.
NOT IMPORTANT	NOT IMPORTANT, BUT URGENT • ANSWERING THE PHONE. • REPLYING TO MOST E-MAILS. • RESPONDING TO FACEBOOK MESSAGES.	NOT IMPORTANT OR URGENT • WATCHING TELEVISION. • CHECKING SOCIAL MEDIA. • BROWSING THE INTERNET.

The great thing about this matrix is how widely applicable it is. You can use it as you plan out your year, day, or next hour. No matter the time frame, it helps you filter out the noise so you can focus your limited time, energy, and attention where it truly matters.

Connecting it to the mental models we've covered so far, the Eisenhower Matrix helps you uncover your 80/20 tasks, stay within your circle of competence, and reduce the opportunity costs that come with doing what's urgent instead of important.

So as you decide what to do next, ask yourself, "Is this important or urgent?" If it's truly important, go ahead and do it now or schedule it for later. But if it's just urgent, try to delegate or delete it altogether.

That way, you'll make more efficient choices, minimize unnecessary stress, and increase your productivity.

7. FIRST PRINCIPLES THINKING

*Breaking down problems into their basic
parts and reassembling them.*

In 2002, technology entrepreneur Elon Musk began his mission to send the first rocket to Mars. And right away, he ran into a major problem.

After visiting several aerospace manufacturers around the world, he found that the cost of a rocket was enormous—as much as $65 million.

But he didn't let that faze him. Instead, he started to rethink his approach. In an interview with *Wired*,[57] he said:

> *I tend to approach things from a physics framework. And physics teaches you to reason from first principles rather than by analogy. So I said, OK, let's look at the first principles. What is a rocket made of? Aerospace-grade aluminum alloys, plus some titanium, copper, and carbon fiber. And then I asked, what is the value of those materials on the commodity market? It turned out that the materials cost of a rocket was around 2 percent of the typical price.*

Instead of getting a ready-made rocket, Musk decided to create his own company, buy the cheap raw materials, and build it himself. And within just a few years, his company SpaceX had cut the cost of launching a rocket by almost ten times while still making a profit.

First principles thinking means breaking down complicated problems into basic elements and then reassembling them from the ground up. It's one of the most powerful ways to learn how to think for yourself, unlock your creativity, and come up with innovative ideas.

Few of us approach our problems that way. Instead, we reason by analogy, relying on prior assumptions, beliefs, and widely held "best practices" to build knowledge and solve problems. And while that requires less mental energy, it also gets us stuck in existing conventions.

How can you use first principles thinking in your life? Here is Elon Musk's three-step process:[58]

Step 1: Identify and define your current assumptions.

Step 2: Break down the problem into its fundamental principles.

Step 3: Create new solutions from scratch.

Since most of us aren't building space rockets anytime soon, let's apply this process to a more relatable problem. Let's say, for example, that you're struggling to find the time to work out. To solve that problem, your steps might look something like this:

1) Working out requires me to go to the gym and, with my busy schedule, there's just no time for that.

2) To increase my fitness, all I really have to do is work out at a level that my body isn't used to.

3) I could try a quick high-intensity interval training routine like the seven-minute workout.

Working out doesn't require a lot of time at the gym. But if you rely on reasoning by analogy, it's easy to forget about that.

And that's why first principles thinking is so useful. It helps you shake off prior assumptions so you can find more innovative solutions.

So, whenever you face a complicated problem, try breaking it down and reassembling it. That way, you'll step outside conventional wisdom and see what's truly possible.

8. SECOND-LEVEL THINKING

Identifying subsequent consequences before they happen.

In his book *The Most Important Thing*, investor Howard Marks explains the difference between first- and second-level thinking:[59]

> *First-level thinking is simplistic and superficial, and just about everyone can do it (a bad sign for anything involving an attempt at superiority). All the first-level thinker needs is an opinion about the future, as in "The outlook for the company is favorable, meaning the stock will go up." Second-level thinking is deep, complex and convoluted.*

First-level thinkers look for answers that are quick and easy. Second-level thinkers look for solutions at the second, third, and nth order.

The ability to move past first-level thinking is crucial to avoid poor decisions and costly mistakes. That's because second-level thinking is how you identify the consequences of a decision before they happen.

Consider, for example, the introduction of the cane toad in Australia. In 1935, about 3,000 of these warty amphibians were released in the sugarcane plantations in north Queensland with the hope that they would hunt and kill cane-destroying beetles in the area.

Unfortunately, the cane toads turned out to be bad beetle hunters, partly because the cane fields provide inadequate shelter during the day, and partly because the beetles live at the tops of sugar canes, and the toads are bad climbers.

They have, however, been remarkably successful at reproducing and spreading themselves. Today, there are millions, if not billions, of cane toads in Australia. Their still-expanding range covers thousands of square miles in the northeastern part of the country.

And while they haven't been effective in reducing beetles, they've had marked effects in other parts of Australia's ecology. Examples include the depletion of native species, the poisoning of pets and humans, depletion of native fauna, and reduced prey populations for native insectivores, such as skinks.

Because of all that, cane toads are now considered pests themselves, and government eradication efforts include asking residents to help collect and dispose of them.[60]

Whoops. First-level thinking: These toads will kill the pests we hate. Second-level thinking: These toads have few natural predators here, they breed easily, and they'll have abundant food. They will become the pests.

The takeaway? When you're facing a complex problem or difficult decision, think deeply about the knock-on effects of each solution or option. Howard Marks outlines his process for second-level thinking as a series of questions like:[61]

- *What is the range of likely future outcomes?*
- *Which outcome do I think will occur?*
- *What's the probability I'm right?*
- *What does the consensus think?*
- *How does my expectation differ from the consensus?*

By digging deeper than the first level, and carefully evaluating what you find at the levels below, you can spot negative consequences before they arise. And that will help you make better decisions and avoid serious mistakes.

9. INVERSION

Thinking backward instead of forward.

During his career, the German mathematician Carl Jacobi made important contributions to several scientific fields. In his work, he often solved difficult problems by following his maxim "man muss immer umkehren," which loosely translates into "invert, always invert."[62]

Jacobi believed that one of the best ways to clarify your thinking is to restate problems in their inverse form. He would write down the opposite of the math problems he was trying to solve and found that the solutions often came more easily to him.

While Jacobi mainly applied inversion to mathematics, it's an equally powerful approach in other areas. No matter what problems you're trying to solve, it can help you uncover errors and roadblocks that aren't readily apparent.

The way to use inversion is to think about things backward instead of forward. Rather than asking how to do something, you ask how *not* to do it. Let's have a look at some examples of what those questions might look like.

Career

- What kind of work feels uninteresting and meaningless to me?
- What is outside my circle of competence?
- What industries have low or decreasing demand?

Business

- What would alienate our core customer?

- How can we become less innovative?
- How can we create a negative company culture?

Productivity

- How can I waste more time on distractions?
- How can I shatter my focus every day?
- How can I reduce the energy I bring to my work?

Health

- How can I decrease the quality and quantity of my sleep?
- What foods can I eat more of to lower my energy and increase the risk of disease?
- How can I make sure I move less every day?

Relationships

- How can I be a bad friend?
- How can I be a terrible leader?
- How can I ruin my marriage?

If you're like most people, you rarely ask yourself questions like these. For most of us, inversion is highly counterintuitive. Thinking backward is not something that comes naturally to us.

But it's very much worth practicing because it helps improve your understanding of problems. It forces you to step out of your status quo bias, consider different perspectives, and come up with new options.

Inverting problems won't always solve them, but it will help you avoid trouble. When you know what you don't want, you can take steps to make sure those things don't happen. And that will move you closer to the solution.

So, whenever the best path forward isn't clear, flip the problem on its head. Instead of trying to find the right path to take, make sure you know which ones to avoid.

Keep in mind: "Invert, always invert."

Spend less time trying to be smart and more time trying to avoid being stupid. Avoiding mistakes is generally much easier than seeking excellence—and it's usually a much better way to solve your problems.

10. BAYESIAN THINKING

Estimating probabilities using prior knowledge.

Thomas Bayes was an eighteenth-century English statistician, philosopher, and minister. His most famous work was "An Essay towards Solving a Problem in the Doctrine of Chances," which he never published himself. Instead, it was introduced to the Royal Society two years after his death by his friend Richard Price.

The essay contained the seeds of what today is called Bayes Theorem, which "describes the probability of an event, based on prior knowledge of conditions that might be related to the event."[63]

If you're not into math, don't worry. You don't have to understand exactly how probability calculations work to benefit from Bayesian thinking. You just have to grasp the intuitions behind the math, which is easy to do. Consider, for example, the following news headline: **Violent Crime Doubles**

If you read that in your local newspaper, you might get worried that your chances of being assaulted have increased dramatically. But is that really true? To find out, we'll use Bayesian thinking to put this new piece of information into the context of your prior knowledge.

Let's say that violent crime in your city has been declining steadily for decades. You know that the risk of being assaulted last year was 1 in 10,000. Since then, according to the news article, violent crime has doubled. That means the risk of assault is now 2 in 10,000. In other words, the risk of getting assaulted is no longer 0.01 percent, but 0.02 percent.

So the headline actually shouldn't make you too worried. Sure, the probability of getting assaulted has increased. It has indeed doubled. But it's still very unlikely to happen. And that's difficult to discern unless you factor in prior information about the situation.

This example illustrates the big idea behind Bayes Theorem: that we should continuously update our probability estimates about things as we come across new information. And that's very different from how we typically approach the world. Usually, we tend to either completely dismiss new evidence or embrace it as though nothing else matters.

As an example of that, let's say that you consider yourself a good driver. But then, one day, you get into a car accident. In that situation, most people will either protect their belief ("It was the other guy's fault") or replace it altogether ("I guess I'm a terrible driver").

By instead using Bayesian thinking, you look at the situation in the context of your prior experience. Sure, the car accident is evidence against your theory that you're a good driver. But that doesn't mean you stubbornly have to protect or immediately replace that belief. It just means you should be a little less confident that it's accurate.

Instead of being 100 percent or 0 percent sure that your theory is correct, you assign it a more reasonable probability. If you've been driving for ten years with no prior accidents, perhaps you can now be 90 percent sure that you're a good driver. With that estimate in mind, you don't have to avoid driving, but you might want to be a little more cautious than you were previously.

Reasoning this way makes you much more aware that your beliefs are grey scale rather than black and white. It allows you to continually update the level of confidence in your own theories about the world. And that helps you make more accurate predictions, improve your decisions, and get better outcomes.

11. MULTIPLYING BY ZERO

Anything times zero is always zero.

In 1986, college basketball prodigy Leonard "Len" Bias was selected as the second overall pick in the NBA Draft by the Boston Celtics. It seemed like he had everything needed to become one of the best basketball players in the world.

- He was 6 ft 9 in (2.06 m), incredibly skillful, and amazingly athletic.

- He lived in Maryland, a place that reveres basketball, and had great support from his parents.

- He had a proven track record, getting two Atlantic Coast Conference Player of the Year awards and named into two All-American teams.

There was just one problem. Bias had developed a cocaine habit, and two days after they picked him in the NBA draft, he passed away from an overdose.

Today, many sportswriters consider Bias to be the greatest basketball player who never played professionally.[64] And what his tragic destiny illustrates is a simple rule we've all learned in math class: anything times zero is always zero. It doesn't matter what the other numbers are—if you multiply them by zero, the answer will inevitably also be zero.

$$1 \times 0 = 0$$

$$128 \times 16 \times 0 = 0$$

$$1{,}577{,}404 \times 99{,}503 \times 6.76 \times 0 = 0$$

Len Bias had incredibly high "numbers" in terms of talent, support, and track record. But in the end, none of that mattered because as soon as he added the "zero" of his cocaine addiction to the equation, the end result was zero.

That's the profound insight behind this simple mathematical fact: all of your talent and hard work can be eradicated entirely by just one weak link in the chain. Let's have a look at some examples.

- You can have everything working for you in your career—a great education, an excellent resume, and an impressive background—but none of that matters if you can't deal with other people.

- Your company might seem impressive—big-name investors, large offices, fancy systems, tons of employees, and a great product or service—but it'll still struggle to be profitable if your customer service is terrible.

- You can get every productivity tool on the market—fancy apps for project management, communication, time-tracking, note-making, and email management—but that won't help you if you're constantly distracted by email and social media.

- You can have plenty of healthy habits—get regular exercise, eat healthy, and meditate every morning—but if you're not sleeping sufficiently, you'll still have an increased risk of cancer, heart attack, and Alzheimer's disease.

- You can be an excellent partner in pretty much every aspect—a great listener, accepting, supportive, and fun to be with—but your relationship can still fall apart if you spend too much time at work.

No matter what you want to accomplish, examine the most critical factors in getting there. Tease out and strengthen the weakest part of the chain. That way, you'll ensure all your hard work isn't for nothing.

12. OCCAM'S RAZOR

The simplest solution tends to be the right one.

William of Occam was a fourteenth-century English friar, philosopher, and theologian. He's considered one of the prominent figures of medieval thought and was involved in many major intellectual and political controversies during his time.

William is most commonly known for the methodological principle called Occam's razor.[65] He did not coin the term himself, but his way of reasoning inspired other thinkers to develop it.

Occam's razor is basically a rule of thumb for problem-solving which states, "Among competing hypotheses, the one with the fewest assumptions should be selected." Another way of putting it is that the simplest solution is probably correct.

Using Occam's razor, you "cut away" what's excessively complex so you can focus on what works. This approach is used in a wide range of situations to improve judgment and support better decisions. To understand how, let's have a look at a few examples.

Science

Many great scientists have used Occam's razor in their work. Albert Einstein is one of them. His version of the same principle was "Everything should be made as simple as possible, but not simpler." This preference for simplicity shows in his famous equation $E=MC^2$. Rather than settling for a complex, lengthy equation, Einstein boiled it down to its bare minimum.

Medicine

Medical interns are often instructed: "When you hear hoofbeats, think of horses, not zebras." The underlying idea is to always consider obvious explanations for symptoms before turning to more unlikely diagnoses. This version of Occam's razor helps physicians reduce the risk of overtreating patients or causing dangerous interactions between different treatments.

Crime

By using a combination of statistical knowledge and experience, Occam's razor can be used in solving crimes. For example, women are statistically more likely to be killed by a male partner than anyone else. So, if a woman is found in her locked home murdered, the first person to look for is any male partners. By focusing on the most likely perpetrators first, the police can solve crime more efficiently.

As a mental model, Occam's razor works best for making initial conclusions with limited information. To use it, you compare the complexity of different options and favor the simplest one.

Imagine, for example, that you come home one day and find that your living room window is open. This surprises you, as you're usually very diligent in closing it. There are two possible explanations for this:

1) You had a lot on your mind when you left and forgot to close it.

2) Someone has broken into your home while you were away.

The first explanation only requires a little mindlessness on your part. The second explanation, however, means someone had to open your window from the outside, disarm your alarm, avoid detection by neighbors, clean up behind them, and leave just as quietly as they came. Therefore, in the absence of any evidence to the contrary, the first explanation is the simplest and the most likely to be correct.

Occam's razor obviously isn't perfect. There are exceptions to every rule, and you should never follow them blindly. But, in general, favoring the simple over the complex will improve your judgment and help you solve problems faster and better.

13. HANLON'S RAZOR

Never attribute to malice that which can be
adequately explained by neglect.

Do you ever feel like the world is against you? If so, you are not alone. We all tend to assume that when things go wrong, it's because the people in our lives are conspiring against us.

Your colleague didn't tell you about an important meeting? He must be trying to make you look bad and beat you to the promotion. Your friends met up without inviting you? They must be going behind your back because they don't like you anymore. Your kids put finger paint all over your kitchen wall? They must be trying to drive you insane.

But in reality, these explanations aren't likely to be true. It's much more probable that your colleague simply forgot to tell you, that your friends assumed you were busy, and that your kids have yet to learn the difference between a kitchen wall and a canvas. And that's why Hanlon's razor is such a handy tool.

Hanlon's razor is an adage, coined by Robert J. Hanlon, which is best summarized as "Never attribute to malice that which can be adequately explained by neglect." It's essentially a special case of Occam's razor which, as we covered in the last chapter, states, "Among competing hypotheses, the one with the fewest assumptions should be selected."

In a situation where something can be explained either by malice or neglect, the latter is more likely. Malice is a big assumption, but negligence is not. People rarely have genuinely bad intentions, but they make mistakes all the time. And by applying Hanlon's razor in our interactions with others, we can negate the effects of many of our cognitive biases. For example:

The Fundamental Attribution Error

We tend to blame the mistakes of others on their personality, and our own mistakes on the circumstances. If someone else is driving too fast, it's because they're an inconsiderate idiot. But if we're the one who's speeding, it's because the situation warrants it. Hanlon's razor helps us assign situational reasons to everyone's mistakes—not just our own.

The Availability Bias

We often misjudge the frequency of recent events, especially if they're vivid and memorable. Many of us keep a mental scorecard of other people's mistakes. When a new mistake is made, it's magnified by errors in the past, and we start to imagine malicious intent. Hanlon's razor helps us see each mistake as an isolated occurrence.

The Confirmation Bias

We have a tendency to seek out information that confirms our preexisting beliefs. If we expect malicious intent, we are likely to attribute it whenever possible. Hanlon's razor helps us stop looking for confirming evidence so we can accurately identify honest mistakes.

So, whenever you feel mistreated, keep in mind: "Never attribute to malice that which can be adequately explained by neglect." It will make you less judgmental and more empathetic. You'll be able to give other people the benefit of the doubt. And that will make for better relationships and a lot less stress.

Of course, there are people out there who do have malicious intent, and that needs to be taken into account. You don't want to be blind to behavior that is intended to be harmful. But, as a rule of thumb, assuming neglect before malice will make you more accurate in your judgments—and a better fellow human.

14. INCENTIVES

Things that motivate someone to do something.

At the time of French colonial rule of Hanoi, Vietnam, the government was worried about the number of rats in the city, so they created a bounty program that paid a reward for every rat killed. The arrangement was simple: provide a severed rat tail, and you'll get a bounty.

It seemed like a decent enough incentive system. But soon, colonial officials noticed something peculiar—rats without tails started to show up in Hanoi.

In a striking demonstration of the importance of second-level thinking, rat hunters would capture rats, sever their tails, and set them free. That way, the rats could procreate and increase the revenue of the rat hunters.

The government had requested rat tails, and they got exactly what they asked for. But in the process, they motivated the wrong behavior and failed miserably in achieving their intended goal. And that makes the Great Hanoi Rat Hunt[66] a great example of an incentive system gone awry.

The takeaway here is that incentives matter a lot. They lie at the root of many situations we face, and yet we often fail to account for them. To get a deeper and more structured understanding of incentives, we'll turn to behavioral psychology.

If we like the consequences of an action we've taken, we're more likely to do it again. And if we don't like the consequences of an action we've taken, we're less likely to do it again.

That's the basic assumption behind what psychologists call operant conditioning: "a learning process through which the strength of a behavior is modified by reinforcement or punishment."[67]

If you want to change behavior, there are two primary tools at your disposal, reinforcement, which strengthens the behavior, and punishment, which weakens the behavior.

Research shows that consistency and timing are crucial for reinforcement. The best way to learn a new behavior is through continuous reinforcement, in which the behavior is reinforced every time it occurs. Meanwhile, the best way to maintain an already established behavior is through intermittent reinforcement, in which the behavior is reinforced only some of the time.

Let's say that you want to teach your dog to sit. Initially, the best strategy is to reward every successful attempt. Later, when your dog knows how to sit, it's better to reward it sometimes.

Punishment has several issues that generally make it less effective than reinforcement. Firstly, behavior tends to return when the punishment is removed. Secondly, punishment tends to lead to increased fear, stress, and aggression. And thirdly, punishment is a poor guide because it doesn't tell you what to do—only what not to do.

So when you feel tempted to punish a behavior, remember that it's usually more effective to manipulate the reinforcers involved instead.

If you want to stop your dog from begging for food, it's a good strategy to ignore every attempt (no matter how cute) and instead reward it when it doesn't beg.

You generally get the behavior you reward, so whenever you want to change behavior, carefully consider the reinforcers in play. Create an effective incentive system, and the desired behavior will follow.

15. NUDGING

*Subtle cues or context changes that gently
push you toward a certain decision.*

In their book, *Nudge*, Richard H. Thaler and Cass R. Sunstein explain that small and seemingly insignificant details in the environment can have a big impact on people's choices and behaviors:

"A wonderful example of this principle comes from, of all places, the men's rooms at Schiphol Airport in Amsterdam. There the authorities have etched the image of a black housefly into each urinal. It seems that men usually do not pay much attention to where they aim, which can create a bit of a mess, but if they see a target, attention and therefore accuracy is much increased."[68]

The result? According to economist Aad Kieboom, who came up with the urinal fly idea, these simple etchings reduce spillage by 80 percent!

That's a remarkable result and a great illustration of the power of "nudging:" small, simple, and inexpensive changes to the environment that increase the likelihood that people will make certain choices or behave in particular ways. Researchers have found several effective nudging techniques, including:

- Default option—People are more likely to choose whatever is presented as the default option. For example, one study found that more consumers chose renewable energy for electricity when it was offered as the default choice.[69]

- Social proof—People tend to look to the behavior of other people to help guide their own. Studies have found that leveraging that tendency can be a helpful way to nudge people into making healthier food choices.[70]

- Salience—People are more likely to choose options that are more noticeable than others. For example, one study found that snack shop consumers buy more fruit and healthy snacks when those options are placed right next to the cash register.[71]

The beauty of nudging is that it allows you to make smarter decisions and take better actions without even thinking about them. You simply shape your environment and then let your environment shape your decisions. Here are some examples of how you can use this strategy in your life:

- If you want to start flossing, put pre-made flossers in a cup next to your toothbrush.

- If you want to practice the guitar more often, place your guitar stand next to your living room couch.

- If you want to lose weight, store away your big plates and serve yourself on salad plates instead.

- If you want to read more, put a great book right on top of your favorite pillow.

- If you want to be more productive, use an app like Freedom to block distracting websites.

We tend to assume that good decisions require conscious effort, and that healthy behaviors require strong willpower. But often, all you need is a slight nudge in the right direction, and the rest will take care of itself. So take a look at your environment and ask yourself, "How can I make good choices easy and bad choices difficult?"

16. CONFORMITY

*Matching attitudes, beliefs, and behaviors
to the norms of the group.*

In the 1950s, psychologist Solomon Asch conducted a series of experiments to investigate the power of social pressure.[72] At the start of each experiment, a participant entered a room with a group of strangers. The subject didn't know it, but these people were actors pretending to play the other participants.

The group was then given a simple task. First, they were shown a card with a single line on it and a second card with a series of lines. Each person was asked to point out the line on the second card that was the same length as the line on the first card.

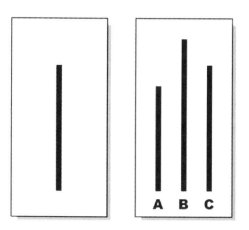

Initially, there were some easy trials where the entire group agreed on the same line. But after a few rounds, the actors would deliberately select what was obviously an incorrect answer. The bewildered subject then had to decide whether to trust their own judgment or conform to the group.

Asch ran this experiment several times in many different ways. And what he found was that as he increased the number of actors, the conformity of the subject also increased. One or two other "participants" had little impact. But as the number of actors increased to three, four, and all the way up to eight, the subject became more likely to give the same answer as everyone else.

Overall, 75 percent of participants gave an incorrect answer at least once. In the control group, where there was no pressure to conform to actors, the same error rate was less than 1 percent.

How could that be? Well, human beings are social creatures with a deep need for belonging. The reward of being accepted is usually greater than the reward of being accurate. So, for the most part, we'd rather be wrong in a group than right by ourselves.

As a species, we are ill-equipped to live on our own, so the human mind has evolved to get along with others. Because of that, we experience tremendous internal pressure to comply with the norms of the group. And, as a result, we tend to conform to those around us.

It's a natural thing to do, and there's nothing inherently wrong with it. But there can be severe downsides to this tendency. If you're not mindful of it, your intentions can get consistently overpowered by the prevailing group norms.

Consider, for instance, sleeping habits. Insufficient sleep ruins your health, performance, and well-being. Still, at least 50 percent of American adults are chronically sleep-deprived. And this devastating trend of sleeping too little is taking place throughout the industrialized world.[73]

There's a prevailing norm that sleep is a luxury rather than a necessity. And as the surrounding people conform to it, you'll likely do it, too.

If something seems like the normal thing to do, you'll naturally gravitate toward it—regardless of the outcome.

So make sure to surround yourself with people who consistently make the choices you want to make. Soon, the way they do things will become the way you do things.

17. EVOLUTION BY NATURAL SELECTION

The organisms best adapted to their environment tend to thrive.

In the nineteenth century, Charles Darwin and Alfred Russel Wallace simultaneously had what's been called "the greatest idea anyone ever had." They both independently realized that species evolve through random mutation and differential survival rates.

Those best suited for survival in their environment tend to be preserved. This process, where Mother Nature decides the success or failure of particular mutations, is called "natural selection."[74]

To understand how it works, imagine a population of red beetles living in a garden. Birds can spot and eat them pretty easily. But one day, a random mutation—a small change in genetic instructions—occurs, and a green baby beetle is born.

Purely by chance, the green beetle is nearly impossible for the birds to see. Thanks to its accidental camouflage, it can survive, reproduce, and pass on its genes more easily than the red beetles.

As a result, the green color becomes increasingly common in the population. And if this process continues, eventually, all the beetles in the garden will be green.

After reading Charles Darwin's *The Origin of Species*, English philosopher Herbert Spencer used the term "survival of the fittest" to describe natural selection. This expression is still widely used today and often misunderstood.

Many people think "fittest" means the best physical specimen of the species and that only those in the best shape will survive in nature.

But that's not always the case. "Fittest," in this context, simply means the one best suited for the immediate environment.

And that idea applies in many other areas outside biology. Businesses, for example, are subject to their own kind of evolutionary arms races. To survive, a company constantly needs to adapt to an ever-evolving world and continually changing marketplace.

The video rental industry provides a great illustration of that. When Netflix launched in 1997, Blockbuster was the undisputed champion of their field. Between 1985 and 1992, the brick-and-mortar rental chain had expanded from its first location in Dallas, Texas, to over 2,800 locations around the world.

By the time Netflix came along with their rental-by-mail service, it looked like a classic David versus Goliath scenario. Still, they upended the video rental industry from day one. They had no late fees or shipping charges. If you lost a DVD, you got a new one in the mail with no questions asked.

Blockbuster tried to follow suit, matching service for service, but it was too late. In 2010 they filed for bankruptcy. Meanwhile, Netflix is still evolving, having gone from sending DVDs by mail, to streaming of other's content, to now streaming of their own content.

Their ability to adapt quickly to the ever-changing needs and preferences of their customers makes Netflix the "fittest" in their industry. Much like the green beetle in the garden, they are the ones best suited for their environment.

Evolution by natural selection is useful to understand because it explains what it takes to survive and thrive. To be successful, you need to embrace change. You have to pay attention to the ever-changing environment and rapidly adapt to it. If you do that, you can gain a critical advantage that puts you way ahead of the competition.

18. HOMEOSTASIS

The tendency of a system to maintain internal stability.

What's the temperature where you are right now? Most likely, it's not precisely 98.6°F (37.0°C). Still, your body temperature is probably very close to that value.

In fact, if your core body temperature doesn't stay within a narrow range—from about 95°F (35.0°C) to 107°F (41.7°C)—the results can be dangerous or even deadly.

So, as you're reading this, every cell in your body and brain are working to maintain a sense of stability. Not just in your core body temperature but also in blood pressure, heart rate, pH balance, blood glucose levels, and many other factors critical to your survival.

This tendency to maintain internal stability—this resistance to change—is called homeostasis, and the human body is just one example of where it takes place. In his book *Mastery*, George Leonard writes:

> *[Homeostasis] characterizes all self-regulating systems, from a bacterium to a frog to a human individual to a family to an organization to an entire culture—and it applies to psychological states and behavior as well as to physical functioning.*[75]

Psychologically, we maintain homeostasis through mental patterns like the status quo bias—our tendency to prefer that things stay as they already are. Socially, we remain stable through forces like conformity—our propensity to maintain attitudes, beliefs, and behaviors congruent with the group.

Imagine, as an example, that for the last ten years or so, you've been almost entirely sedentary. But then, one day, you decide to go for a run. The first few steps are enjoyable, but that quickly changes. After a couple of minutes, you feel light-headed. Moments later, you feel sick to your stomach. And if you keep going, soon enough, you'll feel like if you don't stop, you might just drop dead.

These symptoms are essentially homeostatic alarm signals. Your body has detected changes in respiration, heart rate, and metabolism that are way outside the normal range. To bring them back, your body screams at you: *"Warning! Warning! Whatever you're doing, stop it immediately, or you're going to die!"*

And that's just one way that homeostasis gets in the way of your new fitness goal. On a psychological level, you'll probably experience resistance every time you think about putting on your running shoes. And on a social level, your sedentary friends might not welcome your new exercise habit.

Needless to say, homeostasis makes it difficult to create change. It's a powerful force that often results in backsliding. But the good news is that if you keep pushing, homeostasis will eventually adapt to the new load and create a new set point.

If you keep showing up at the trail, your body will eventually get used to the running, and even begin to crave it. Being a runner will become part of your self-image, and you'll experience resistance if you *don't* go running. And, with time, your friends will get used to this crazy habit of yours—and some of them might even join you.

So whenever you make a decision that requires a big change, expect homeostasis to kick in. Know that there will be backsliding and keep on pushing. Eventually, homeostasis will adapt and start working for you. And from that point forward, it will be much easier.

19. FIGHT OR FLIGHT

The instinctive physiological response to a threatening situation.

Imagine that you're a member of a nomadic tribe of hunter-gatherers living somewhere in North America during the Ice Age. You're out pursuing a bison when, suddenly, a sabre-tooth tiger jumps out in front of you.

At the sight of this threatening environmental stimulus, your body immediately launches into what's called the fight-or-flight response. Stress hormones flood the body and create physiological changes like:[76]

- Increased blood flow to activated muscles by diverting blood from other parts of the body.

- Higher blood pressure, heart rate, blood sugars, and fats to supply the body with a boost of energy.

- Faster blood clotting function to prevent excessive blood loss in case of injury.

- Greater muscle tension to provide the body with extra speed and strength.

These changes help you attack quickly or run like crazy. And if you're standing face-to-face with a sabre-tooth tiger, that's a very helpful reaction. The fight-or-flight response helped our ancestors stay alive, so we inherited it from them.

And while it's still useful, it can also be problematic. Our bodies don't distinguish well between threats to our survival and everyday stressors. So an angry boss, a challenging deadline, or an overwhelming workload can all set off the fight-or-flight response.

And when that happens, your ability to think is also affected. During the fight-or-flight response, your brain has increased activity in areas like the limbic system, which is associated with emotions. Meanwhile, it has decreased activity in areas like the prefrontal cortex, which is associated with decision-making.[77]

In the terms of Daniel Kahneman, you switch from the reflective System 2 to the reflexive System 1. And, as we've covered in a previous chapter, that means you become more susceptible to cognitive biases and logical fallacies. As a result, you're more likely to make hasty decisions based on habitual responses rather than deep thinking.

To be a good decision-maker, you need to be able to face the inevitable stressors of life without getting swept away by the fight-or-flight response. And the best way to do that is to proactively build your stress resilience and deliberately calm down before making important decisions.

Look after your most basic self-care needs. Get sufficient sleep, eat healthy foods, and be physically active every day. That will give your body and brain the rest, fuel, and outlet it needs to cope with the stress that it's experiencing. Prepare well and you'll perform well.

And whenever a big decision arises, take the time to breathe deeply, slow down, and concentrate. Make sure to switch from System 1 to System 2. Then use your mental model checklist to consider what's in front of you from different perspectives.

The less stressed you are, the clearer you'll think, and the better decisions you'll make.

20. ENTROPY

The tendency of everything to move from order to disorder.

The second law of thermodynamics states that "as one goes forward in time, the net entropy (degree of disorder) of any isolated or closed system will always increase (or at least stay the same)."[78]

That's basically a long way of saying that all things tend to move from order to disorder. This is one of the fundamental laws of the universe, and you can see its effects everywhere.

As a simple example, imagine that you walk into a café and order a cup of coffee. Normally, we don't think twice about a simple cup of coffee, but there's actually a lot of time and effort that's gone into it.

The barista reaches for a cup he has cleaned and someone else has made. He then pours water that a power company has heated over coffee beans that got there due to the work of many people. Airplanes, ships, and trucks burned fuel to get them to the café, as well.

Once you get the cup of coffee in your hand, it's a highly ordered structure in the universe. Its entropy is low.

Now, instead of drinking it, imagine what would happen if you just let it sit on the table for 30 minutes. After a while it gets cold. The heat energy moves from the cup and out into the room. That's a gain in entropy.

If you leave the cup for several days, some of the water you paid for will evaporate. It will move from the cup and turn into water vapor in the room. That's another gain in entropy.

Let the cup sit for years, and the material it's made of will eventually break down and fall apart. This, too, is yet another gain in entropy.

It's the natural tendency of all things to lose order. Left to their own devices, everything will become less structured. Gardens get weeds. Cars rust. People age. Civilizations fall. Ancient ruins crumble. Even great mountains gradually erode and disappear.

And the same relentless force is present in all areas of your life. If you don't move your body, you'll lose muscle mass. If you don't answer your emails, your in-box will flood. If you don't nurture your relationships, they will eventually die out.

But the good news is that it's possible to fight back against entropy. The barista can clean the cup and get it ready for the next customer. And you can expend the energy needed to maintain order in your life. It's hard, but also meaningful, work. As psychologist Steven Pinker puts it:

> *"The Second Law of Thermodynamics defines the ultimate purpose of life, mind, and human striving: to deploy energy and information to fight back the tide of entropy and carve out refuges of beneficial order."*[79]

Knowing that everything naturally moves from order to disorder, you can deliberately simplify your life. Let go of everything unimportant so you can spend your limited energy where it truly matters. Carefully choose the areas where you want to fight entropy and tend to them consistently.

Not only will it make you more focused and efficient, but also happier and more fulfilled.

21. MARGIN OF SAFETY

The ability to withstand challenges that are greater than expected.

Imagine that you're an engineer building a bridge. You know that, on an average day, the bridge will need to support about 10,000 tons of traffic at any given time. Would you build it to withstand exactly that weight?

Hopefully, your answer is "no." What if your estimates or calculations are slightly off? What if the bridge gets heavier traffic than average on certain days? What if your building materials are weaker than expected?

To account for all that, you decide to build a bridge that comfortably supports 50,000 tons. In engineering terms, the additional 40,000 ton capacity is a "margin of safety." It's the ability of your bridge to withstand challenges greater than expected.[80]

And that principle is very useful, not just in construction and engineering, but in many areas of life. Let's have a look at some examples.

Time Management

If you're always running late, it's because you're living your life without a sufficient margin of safety. The planning fallacy makes you overoptimistic, and you perpetually overlook that life is full of unexpected delays. To overcome that tendency, you can add extra buffer time before each task in your schedule.

Strength Training

If you push yourself to lift as heavy as you possibly can in the gym, you're eliminating your margin of safety. By instead finishing each set with at least one more repetition in you, you can execute every lift with proper form and reduce the risk of injury.

Personal Finance

If you spend every dime you earn each month, you don't have a financial margin of safety. There's no protection for unexpected expenses. Conversely, if you can get by on 90 percent of your income, the remaining 10 percent can provide a helpful financial buffer.

Investing

If you buy a stock because you consider it slightly undervalued, your investment has a poor margin of safety. Predicting the future is extremely difficult, and that's why famous investors like Warren Buffett usually only buy stocks that are excessively underpriced.

Stress Management

If you don't take care of yourself, you won't have a buffer to deal with the inevitable stressors in life. Good habits like sufficient sleep, healthy eating, regular movement, and mindfulness practice provides an emotional margin of safety for unusually bad days.

All information contains some amount of error. The future is uncertain and, as we learned in the last chapter, entropy makes it ever more complicated. By using a margin of safety, you get a cushion that protects against incorrect estimates, unforeseen events, and plain bad luck.

Always account for the hidden errors. Always leave room for the unexpected. Always be stronger than you need to be. That will make you confident and unshakable—even when things get extraordinarily difficult.

22. ANTIFRAGILITY

The ability to benefit from stressors.

In his book *Antifragile*, statistician and philosopher Nassim Nicholas Taleb writes:

> *"Some things benefit from shocks; they thrive and grow when exposed to volatility, randomness, disorder, and stressors and love adventure, risk, and uncertainty. Yet, in spite of the ubiquity of the phenomenon, there is no word for the exact opposite of fragile. Let us call it antifragile."*[81]

Taleb makes the case that people, organizations, and systems can be described in one of three ways: fragile, resilient, or antifragile. To understand the difference between these categories, imagine three packages that are being sent in the mail:

- The first package says "Handle with care." If you're not careful, everything inside the box will break. It's fragile.

- The second package says "Robust." This box can take some hits before the contents inside break. It's resilient.

- The third package says "Handle roughly." The stuff in this one actually gets stronger if you kick it around. It's antifragile.

Here's the takeaway: You don't want to be fragile. At the very least, you want to be resilient. And ideally, you want to be antifragile. Let's look at some ways you can move from fragility to robustness to antifragility in your life:

Follow *Via Negativa*

According to Taleb, "The first step towards antifragility consists in first decreasing downside."[82] You can do that through *via negativa*, which is Latin for "the negative way." Instead of asking yourself what to add to your life, you invert the question and ask yourself what to remove. For example, get out of debt, stop eating junk food, and quit smoking.

Manage Your Stress Response

When a stressor shows up in your life, there are two ways you can perceive it: as a threat or as a challenge. These different views create very different thoughts, emotions, and behaviors.[83] A threat response makes you fragile, while a challenge response makes you antifragile. So, develop a "Bring it on!" mentality, and stress will strengthen you.

Practice Voluntary Discomfort

The Spartan warriors had a creed that stated, "He who sweats more in training bleeds less in war." You can prepare yourself for the battles of life by practicing voluntary hardship. Occasionally take cold showers, live on a tight budget, drink water only, and so on. Get comfortable being uncomfortable, and the inevitable blows of life won't be as devastating.

Create Redundancies

Nature is filled with redundancies. For example, animals have two lungs, two kidneys, and two testicles, even though one of each would do just fine. But since one in a pair of organs can become disabled through disease or trauma, it pays to have a spare. You can use the same strategy to decrease fragility of the systems in your life. Start an emergency fund, have a spare tire in your car, use an external hard drive to back up your work, and so on.

Use the Barbell Strategy

Taleb describes "the barbell strategy" as "a dual attitude of playing it safe in some areas and taking a lot of small risks in others, hence achieving antifragility."[84] For example, you can keep your day job while working on a side hustle at night. If your side hustle doesn't work out, you still have an income stream, but if it does work out, you might create a more fulfilling and profitable career.

Philosopher Friedrich Nietzsche once said, *"That which does not kill us, makes us stronger."* Set yourself up for antifragility, and you'll find that famous quote to be true.

23. NEWTON'S LAWS OF MOTION

Three laws of mechanics describing the motions of objects.

In 1687, Isaac Newton published his revolutionary book, *The Principia: Mathematical Principles of Natural Philosophy*,[85] in which he stated his three laws of motion.

The *Principia* formed the foundation of classical mechanics and is to this day considered one of the most important works in the history of science.

And, as we'll see in this chapter, Newton's laws of motion can be used as helpful models to create progress in our lives.

Let's have a look at the three laws and use my author career as a simple example for each one.

> **The First Law of Motion:** *Objects in motion tend to stay in motion, and objects at rest tend to stay at rest.*

Whenever you're procrastinating on something, you're experiencing the pull of this law firsthand. Objects at rest tend to stay at rest.

Luckily, it works the other way around, too. If you just get started, you'll generally keep going. Objects in motion tend to stay in motion.

When I started writing, I was constantly fighting this law. I only wrote sporadically and, as a result, getting started was a continuous struggle.

It wasn't until I got a regular writing routine down that I could start to benefit from this law.

Over time, writing first thing in the morning has become second nature. My new homeostasis, if you will.

And you can do the same thing in any area where you'd like to make progress. Get moving, and you'll keep going.

The Second Law of Motion: $F=ma$. *Force equals mass times acceleration.*

There is one important takeaway in the $F=ma$ equation. The force, F, is a vector. Vectors have both magnitude (the amount of effort put in) and direction (where that effort is applied).

If you want an object to accelerate in a particular direction, the amount of effort *and* the direction of that effort will both affect the outcome.

So whenever you want to make progress, it's not just about how hard you work (magnitude), but also about where you apply that work (direction).

As a writer, it's not just the number of quality words I write every day (magnitude) that affects the results in my business.

My decisions about whether to work as a freelancer, ghostwriter, or author (direction) are equally important.

As we've learned in a previous chapter, everything we do has an opportunity cost, so make sure that all your hard work is applied in the most beneficial direction.

The Third Law of Motion: For every action, there is an equal and opposite reaction.

Much like this law describes, your progress is a balance of opposing forces in your life.

There are supporting forces like energy, focus, and motivation. And there are opposing forces like fatigue, overwhelm, and discouragement.

Whenever you want to make more progress, you have two options: you can add supporting forces, or you can remove opposing forces.

As a writer, I've added supporting forces like my daily writing routine, a high-quality writing application, and regular contact with other authors. I've also removed opposing forces like email notifications, desktop clutter, and most social media accounts. As a result, the progress I want to make every day now comes much more easily.

Nudge yourself in the right direction, and your behavior will spontaneously adapt.

Whenever you want to create progress in your life, keep these ideas in mind. Get moving, and you'll keep going. Apply your hard work in the most beneficial direction. And modify the opposing forces in your life. Use Newton's laws of motion to your advantage, and they will naturally carry you forward.

24. ALGORITHMS

Well-defined instructions to perform certain tasks.

In his book *Homo Deus*, historian Yuval Noah Harari writes:

> *'Algorithm' is arguably the single most important concept in our world. If we want to understand our life and our future, we should make every effort to understand what an algorithm is, and how algorithms are connected with emotions.*[86]

So, what is an algorithm? The dictionary defines it as "a process or set of rules to be followed in calculations or other problem-solving operations, especially by a computer."

If you've ever wondered how a Tesla can drive itself, the answer is algorithms—millions of them. But there are also more relatable everyday occurrences of algorithms. Each time you bake a cake, for example, the recipe you use is an algorithm.

And, as psychologists have found, you can also use algorithms to program yourself for better decision-making. Psychology professor Peter Gollwitzer refers to this strategy as if-then planning.[87] To use it, all you have to do is fill out this simple formula:

If [situation]–Then I will [behavior].

The beauty of if-then planning is that it forces you to turn vague intentions into clear algorithms.

"I want to eat healthier," becomes *"If I'm buying lunch, then I will order a salad."*

It sounds ridiculously simple, but don't let that fool you. Over 200 scientific studies show that if-then planners are about 300 percent more likely to achieve their goals. The reason it works so exceptionally well, according to psychologist Heidi Grant, is that "Contingencies are built into our neurological wiring. Humans are very good at encoding information in 'If X, then Y' terms, and using those connections (often unconsciously) to guide their behavior."[88]

In other words: much like computers, our minds respond very well to algorithms. If-then plans allow you to act the way you want without thinking, and that saves a lot of mental energy for other decisions. Instead of hesitating and deliberating, you just follow the algorithm whenever the situation arises. Here are some more examples:

- *"I want to move more."* → If I'm at work, then I will take the stairs.

- *"I want to be more productive."* → If I arrive at the office, then I will do two hours of deep work.

- *"I want to improve my relationships."* → If I come home from work, then I will share the best thing that happened to me that day.

- *"I want to be happier"* → If I wake up in the morning, then I will think about one thing I'm grateful for.

- *"I want to make better decisions."* → If I'm making an important decision, then I will review my checklist of mental models.

Instead of relying on vague intentions, purposely install the responses that will lead you to your goals. Think of yourself as a robot and the if-then plans as the algorithms you use to program yourself. It sounds silly, I know, but it's a remarkably effective way of putting good decisions on autopilot.

25. COMPOUNDING

Interest on interest.

Imagine that you're given a choice right now. You can get either $3 million in cash immediately, or a penny that doubles in value every day for the next 30 days. Which option would you choose?

Most people would take the $3 million. Let's say you do that, and I get the penny.

At the outset, you'll have every reason to be happy with your choice. After one week of compounding, my penny is worth a meager 64 cents. After two weeks, it's at a modest $81.92. And after three weeks, I'm still way behind you. Sure, the penny has transformed into a respectable $10,485.76, but that's still not much compared to your $3 million.

But then, a few days into the third week, the magic of compounding starts to show. On day 28, the penny has grown into a remarkable $1,342,177.28. On day 29, I'm right behind you with $2,684,354.56. And on day 30, I finally pull ahead as my stack of cash compounds into an astonishing $5,368,709.12.

Day	Value	Day	Value	Day	Value
1	$0.01	11	$10.24	21	$10,485.76
2	$0.02	12	$20.48	22	$20,971.52
3	$0.04	13	$40.96	23	$41,943.04
4	$0.08	14	$81.92	24	$83,886.08
5	$0.16	15	$163.84	25	$167,772.16
6	$0.32	16	$327.68	26	$335,544.32
7	$0.64	17	$655.36	27	$671,088.64
8	$1.28	18	$1,310.72	28	$1,342,177.28
9	$2.56	19	$2,621.44	29	$2,684,354.56
10	$5.12	20	$5,242.88	30	$5,368,709.12

The compounding penny illustrates something that our brains have a hard time grasping intuitively: small improvements add up to massive changes over time. And this is just as true in life as in finance. In his book *Atomic Habits*, author James Clear explains:[89]

> *"Here's how the math works out: if you can get 1 percent better each day for one year, you'll end up thirty-seven times better by the time you're done. Conversely, if you get 1 percent worse each day for one year, you'll decline nearly down to zero. What starts as a small win or a minor setback accumulates into something much more. Habits are the compound interest of self-improvement."*

Whenever you make a mundane choice, like ordering a salad instead of a hamburger, that single occasion won't make much of a difference. But as you keep repeating the same decisions and actions over weeks, months, and years, they will compound into significant results.

- If you hit the gym for an hour three times a week, and you do this for a week, you won't get any noticeable results (except maybe some soreness). But if you keep showing up just as often for a year, you'll accumulate 156 hours of exercise. That's more than enough to have a significant effect on your health and fitness.

- If you read one good book, that won't make much of an impact on your thinking. But if you read one every month for a year, you'll finish twelve titles. That will equip your mind with plenty of new mental models to improve your thinking.

- If you meditate a couple of times, it probably won't create any lasting changes. But if you do it for 10 minutes each day for a year, you'll have 60+ hours of meditation practice. And that will most likely have considerable positive effects on your health, well-being, and performance.

There is immense power in tiny improvements. Instead of looking for big wins, start small. Focus on getting just one percent better every day. Allow compounding to work its magic and, over time, it will create remarkable outcomes.

PART 5: FINAL WORDS

The chief enemy of good decisions is a lack of sufficient perspectives on a problem.

—Alain de Botton

A Little Wiser Every Day

The British statistician George Box is considered to be one of the great statistical minds of the twentieth century.

In a groundbreaking 1976 paper, he wrote the famous line, "All models are wrong, some are useful."[90]

Box argued that, instead of endlessly debating whether a model is correct in every instance, we should apply it where it's helpful.

For a great illustration of this principle, let's consider the work of Albert Einstein.

All Ideas Are Imperfect

In 1915, Einstein published one of the most remarkable achievements in science to date: the general theory of relativity.[91]

This idea had a profound effect on our understanding of the universe, and the theory has held up remarkably well over the years.

For instance, general relativity predicted the existence of gravitational waves, ripples in space-time, which weren't directly observed until 2015—100 years after Einstein's prediction.

But even the most brilliant of ideas are imperfect. While general relativity explains how the universe works in many situations, it also breaks down in certain extreme scenarios like, inside black holes.

Utility Over Accuracy

According to historian Yuval Noah Harari, "Scientists usually assume that no theory is 100 percent correct. Consequently, truth is a poor test for knowledge. The real test is utility. A theory that enables us to do new things constitutes knowledge."[92]

Einstein's general theory of relativity doesn't work in every instance, but when it's applied in the right areas, it's incredibly useful.

Not only has it dramatically improved our understanding of the universe, but it's also been extremely valuable for practical, everyday purposes.

The GPS in your phone, for example, has to take the effects of relativity into account to give you accurate directions. If it wasn't for Einstein's imperfect idea, your navigation system wouldn't work.

A Framework for Effective Thinking

Just like the general theory of relativity, every idea presented in this book is imperfect. Our minds are puzzling, our decisions are complicated, and there are no "one size fits all" models to make sense of everything.

No cognitive bias explains all the ways our thinking goes wrong. No logical fallacy describes all the ways that our reasoning breaks down. And no mental model offers a perfect tool for every problem we come across.

But together, all of these concepts make up a useful framework for effective thinking. Combined, they provide a helpful understanding of how your cognitive apparatus works and how to use it.

The more you improve that framework, the more versatile and accurate your thinking will become. And that will help you make ever smarter decisions that lead to increasingly better results.

Remove Your Blind Spots

As you approach problems and decisions, you will have certain blind spots. Sometimes, you'll fall victim to a cognitive bias or logical fallacy. Other times, you'll lack the appropriate mental model or use the wrong one.

Thinking is difficult. There is only one way to be rational, but many ways to be irrational. And since that's the case, you'll inevitably make mistakes from time to time.

Your goal shouldn't be to make perfect decisions every single time. That's not realistic, nor helpful. Instead, your goal should be to continually reduce your blind spots.

In other words, don't try to be intelligent; try not to be stupid.

Use The Decision-Making Blueprint Bonus Bundle to get a deep understanding of the concepts in this book. Put your framework solidly in place—and then continuously improve upon it.

Always Get Smarter

Anyone can improve their thinking, but most of us won't put in the effort. It's much easier and more immediately gratifying to zone out, watch TV, or browse social media.

But that won't help you accumulate useful knowledge, expand your mental toolbox, and make better decisions.

So as our journey together comes to an end, I'd like to leave you with the following piece of advice from Charlie Munger:

"Go to bed smarter than when you woke up."[93]

That simple principle will allow wisdom to build up, integrate, and compound at a remarkable rate.

Make a commitment to lifelong learning. Set aside a little time every day for self-education. Fuel your curiosity and seek to get a little bit wiser every day.

Piece by piece, you'll expand your mental framework. Day by day, you'll make better decisions. And little by little, you'll improve the results in all areas of your life.

Download Your Free Bonus Bundle

You've made it to the end of this book. Great job reading all the way through! If you're excited to put everything you've learned to use, I recommend you download your free copy of The Decision-Making Blueprint Bonus Bundle right now.

This companion resource will make it as easy as possible for you to internalize all the concepts covered in this book and use them in your decision-making.

Go here to grab *The Decision-Making Blueprint Bonus Bundle*
https://patrikedblad.com/the-good-life-blueprint-series-bonuses

Acknowledgments

I have relied on a lot of people while creating this book. Before anyone else, I want to thank my girlfriend Lisa who, as always, has provided invaluable guidance and encouragement at every step along the way. Second, I'm deeply grateful for the unceasing support of my family, friends, and peers. And third, to all my wonderful readers for their continuous feedback and supportive messages.

As for the content of the book, I have a long list of brilliant thinkers, educators, and researchers to thank. Daniel Kahneman, Amos Tversky, Dan Ariely, Charlie Munger, Shane Parrish, James Clear, Derek Muller, Gabriel Weinberg, Buster Benson, Bo Bennett, and Kevin deLaplante have all deeply influenced my understanding of decision-making. If you enjoyed this book, I highly recommend you check out their work as well.

To Kristie, Rob, Jordan, Erica, Vanessa, and the rest of the fabulous team at Archangel Ink, thank you for another great collaboration and for making this book a reality. I'm also grateful to the talented Sarah Moore, who designed the beautiful images in this book.

I'm sure there are people I've forgotten, but I keep an updated list of anyone who's influenced my work in meaningful ways at patrikedblad.com/thanks.

And finally, to you. Life is short and there are countless books to choose from. Thank you for sharing some of your precious time with me by reading this book. I hope you found it insightful.

Endnotes

1. "Prospect Theory: An Analysis of Decision under Risk." Jstor. Accessed July 30, 2019. https://www.jstor.org/stable/1914185.

2. "Half of U.S. Adults Would Change at Least One Education Decision." Gallup. Accessed July 30, 2019. https://news.gallup.com/poll /211529/half-adults-change-least-one-education-decision.aspx.

3. "1 in 3 adults don't get enough sleep." CDC Online Newsroom, CDC. Accessed July 30, 2019. https://www.cdc.gov/media/releases/2016/p0215 -enough-sleep.html.

4. "Physical Inactivity: A Global Public Health Problem." WHO. Accessed July 30, 2019. https://www.who.int/dietphysicalactivity/factshe et_inactivity/en/.

5. "Health effects of dietary risks in 195 ...." Lancet. Accessed July 30, 2019. https://www.thelancet.com/article/S0140-6736(19)30041-8/full text.

6. "Marriage and Divorce - American ...." APA. Accessed July 30, 2019. https://www.apa.org/topics/divorce/.

7. *The Top Five Regrets of the Dying: A Life Transformed by the Dearly Departing* by Bronnie Ware: https://www.goodreads.com/book/show/130 59271-the-top-five-regrets-of-the-dying

8. "Largest neuronal network simulation achieved using K computer ...." Riken. Accessed July 30, 2019. http://www.riken.jp/en/pr/press/2013/20 130802_1/.

9. "(PDF) The Evolution of Cognitive Bias." ResearchGate. Accessed July 30, 2019. https://www.researchgate.net/publication/308584925_The _Evolution_of_Cognitive_Bias.

10. "(PDF) Medicine. Do defaults save lives?" ResearchGate. Accessed July 30, 2019. https://www.researchgate.net/publication/8996952_Medicine_Do_defaults_save_lives.

11. "(PDF) On the Failure to Eliminate Hypotheses in a Conceptual Task." Accessed July 30, 2019. https://pdfs.semanticscholar.org/86db/64c600fe59acfc48fd22bc8484485d5e7337.pdf.

12. "Self-serving bias in the classroom: Who shows it? Who knows it?" Accessed July 30, 2019. https://psycnet.apa.org/record/1996-01721-010.

13. "Explanations for unemployment in Britain." Wiley Online Library. Accessed July 30, 2019. https://onlinelibrary.wiley.com/doi/pdf/10.1002/ejsp.2420120402.

14. "(PDF) Attributions in the Sports Pages - ResearchGate." Accessed July 30, 2019. https://www.researchgate.net/publication/232567890_Attributions_in_the_Sports_Pages.

15. *The Better Angels of Our Nature: Why Violence Has Declined* by Steven Pinker: https://www.goodreads.com/book/show/13543093-the-better-angels-of-our-nature

16. *Thinking, Fast and Slow* by Daniel Kahneman, page 8: https://www.goodreads.com/book/show/12385458-thinking-fast-and-slow

17. "Abraham Wald's Work on Aircraft Survivability." ResearchGate. Accessed July 30, 2019. https://www.researchgate.net/publication/254286514_Abraham_Wald's_Work_on_Aircraft_Survivability.

18. Daniel Kahneman: The Trouble with Confidence: https://www.youtube.com/watch?v=tyDQFmA1SpU

19. "The Endowment Effect, Loss Aversion, and Status Quo Bias." ResearchGate. Accessed July 30, 2019. https://www.researchgate.net/profile/Richard_Thaler/publication/4730791_The_Endowment_Effect_Loss_Aversion_and_Status_Quo_Bias/links/09e4151030d3ea82e9000000/The-Endowment-Effect-Loss-Aversion-and-Status-Quo-Bias.pdf.

20. "Status Quo Bias in Decision Making." Accessed October 21, 2019. https://sites.hks.harvard.edu/fs/rzeckhau/status%20quo%20bias.pdf.

21. "(PDF) Medicine. Do defaults save lives?" ResearchGate. Accessed July 30, 2019. https://www.researchgate.net/publication/8996952_Medicine_Do_defaults_save_lives.

22. "Anchoring bias in decision-making." ScienceDaily. Accessed July 30, 2019. https://www.sciencedaily.com/terms/anchoring.htm.

23. "Models of Temporal Discounting 1937–2000: An Interdisciplinary ...." Accessed July 30, 2019. https://people.kth.se/~gryne/papers/Hyperbol_150401.pdf.

24. "Time Discounting and Time Preference: A Critical Review." Universitat Innsbruk. Accessed July 30, 2019. https://www.uibk.ac.at/economics/bbl/lit_se/lit_se_ss06_papiere/time_discounting.pdf.

25. "I'll have the ice cream soon and the vegetables later: A ..." Springer. Accessed July 30, 2019. https://link.springer.com/article/10.1007/s11002-009-9087-0.

26. *The Marshmallow Test: Mastering Self-Control* by Walter Mischel: https://www.goodreads.com/book/show/20454074-the-marshmallow-test

27. "Unskilled and Unaware of It: How Difficulties in ..." Semantic Scholar. Accessed July 30, 2019. https://pdfs.semanticscholar.org/e320/9ca64cbed9a441e55568797cbd3683cf7f8c.pdf.

28. "The Anosognosic's Dilemma." Opinionator - The New York Times. Accessed July 30, 2019. https://opinionator.blogs.nytimes.com/2010/06/20/the-anosognosics-dilemma-1/.

29. "Everyone has a bias blind spot, researchers find." ScienceDaily. Accessed July 30, 2019. https://www.sciencedaily.com/releases/2015/06/150608213028.htm.

30. "Bias Blind Spot: Structure, Measurement, and ..." ResearchGate. Accessed July 30, 2019. https://www.researchgate.net/publication/275723 267_Bias_Blind_Spot_Structure_Measurement_and_Consequences.

31. *Elementary Lessons in Logic: Deductive and Inductive: With Copious Questions and Examples, and a Vocabulary of Logical Terms* by William Stanley Jevons, page 169: https://www.goodreads.com/book/show/21852 80.Elementary_Lessons_In_Logic

32. "(PDF) Medicine. Do defaults save lives?" ResearchGate. Accessed July 30, 2019. https://www.researchgate.net/publication/8996952_Medic ine_Do_defaults_save_lives.

33. "Law Of Large Numbers: Overview." Investopedia. Accessed July 30, 2019. https://www.investopedia.com/terms/l/lawoflargenumbers.asp.

34. *Thinking, Fast and Slow* by Daniel Kahneman, page 113: https://www .goodreads.com/book/show/12385458-thinking-fast-and-slow

35. "Correlation does not imply causation." Semantic Scholar. Accessed July 30, 2019. https://pdfs.semanticscholar.org/d886/674ab022d6d34447 320ed62b96ebab9ead60.pdf.

36. *Spurious Correlations* by Tyler Vigen: https://www.goodreads.com/bo ok/show/23197309-spurious-correlations

37. Full Service Moving Commercial from United Van Lines: https:// www.youtube.com/watch?v=_DMUGabJ8Mw

38. "The psychology of sunk cost." ResearchGate. Accessed July 30, 2019. https://www.researchgate.net/publication/4812596_The_psychology_of _sunk_cost.

39. "It's About Time: Optimistic Predictions in Work and Love." Taylor&Francis Online. Accessed July 30, 2019. https://www.tandfonline .com/doi/pdf/10.1080/1479277934300112.

40. "DENVER INTERNATIONAL AIRPORT Information on …" GovInfo. Accessed July 30, 2019. https://www.govinfo.gov/content/pkg/GAOREPORTS-AIMD-95-230/pdf/GAOREPORTS-AIMD-95-230.pdf.

41. "The Hourglass Is Half Full or Half Empty: Temporal …" APA PsycNET. Accessed July 30, 2019. https://psycnet.apa.org/record/2005-11262-003.

42. "The Hourglass Is Half Full or Half Empty: Temporal …" APA PsycNET. Accessed July 30, 2019. https://psycnet.apa.org/record/2005-11262-003.

43. "People focus on optimistic scenarios and disregard …" ResearchGate. Accessed July 30, 2019. https://www.researchgate.net/publication/12309770_People_focus_on_optimistic_scenarios_and_disregard_pessimistic_scenarios_when_predicting_task_completion_times.

44. "Fallacy fallacy." RationalWiki. Accessed July 30, 2019. https://rationalwiki.org/wiki/Fallacy_fallacy.

45. *Behave: The Biology of Humans at Our Best and Worst* by Robert M. Sapolsky, page 5: https://www.goodreads.com/book/show/31170723-behave

46. *Thinking, Fast and Slow* by Daniel Kahneman, page 20: https://www.goodreads.com/book/show/12385458-thinking-fast-and-slow

47. *Thinking, Fast and Slow* by Daniel Kahneman, page 28: https://www.goodreads.com/book/show/12385458-thinking-fast-and-slow

48. "A Non-Aristotelian System and its Necessity for Rigour in Mathematics and Physics." Accessed July 30, 2019. http://esgs.free.fr/uk/art/sands-sup3.pdf.

49. "The Map Is Not the Territory." Farnam Street." Accessed July 30, 2019. https://fs.blog/2015/11/map-and-territory/.

50. "Cours d'Économie Politique." SAGE Journals. Accessed July 30, 2019. http://journals.sagepub.com/doi/abs/10.1177/00027162970090 0314.

51. *Manual of Political Economy: A Critical and Variorum Edition* by Vilfredo Pareto: https://www.goodreads.com/book/show/22123853-ma nual-of-political-economy

52. "Chairman's Letter – 1996." Berkshire Hathaway Inc. Accessed July 30, 2019. https://www.berkshirehathaway.com/letters/1996.html.

53. "Understanding your Circle of Competence: How Warren Buffett Avoids ...." Farnam Street. Accessed July 30, 2019. https://fs.blog/2013 /12/circle-of-competence/.

54. "The Four Burners Theory: The Downside of Work-Life ...." James Clear. Accessed July 30, 2019. https://jamesclear.com/four-burners-th eory.

55. *Principles of Economics* by N. Gregory Mankiw, page 4: https://www .goodreads.com/book/show/5754642-principles-of-economics

56. "Introducing the Eisenhower Matrix." Accessed July 30, 2019. https://www.eisenhower.me/eisenhower-matrix/.

57. "Elon Musk's Mission to Mars." WIRED. Accessed July 30, 2019. https://www.wired.com/2012/10/ff-elon-musk-qa/.

58. "Elon Musk says he owes his success to a 3-step problem-solving trick ...." Business Insider. Accessed July 30, 2019. https://www.businessi nsider.in/elon-musk-says-he-owes-his-success-to-a-3-step-problem-sol ving-trick-also-used-by-thomas-edison-and-nikola-tesla/articleshow/68 515173.cms.

59. *The Most Important Thing: Uncommon Sense for the Thoughtful Investor* by Howard Marks, page 4: https://www.goodreads.com/book/show/1045 4418-the-most-important-thing

60. "Cane Toad." National Geographic. Accessed July 30, 2019. https://www.nationalgeographic.com/animals/amphibians/c/cane-toad/.

61. *The Most Important Thing: Uncommon Sense for the Thoughtful Investor* by Howard Marks, page 4: https://www.goodreads.com/book/show/10454418-the-most-important-thing

62. "Carl Gustav Jacob Jacobi." Wikipedia. Accessed July 30, 2019. https://en.wikipedia.org/wiki/Carl_Gustav_Jacob_Jacobi.

63. "Bayes' theorem." Wikipedia. Accessed July 30, 2019. https://en.wikipedia.org/wiki/Bayes%27_theorem.

64. "The legend of Len Bias." ESPN.com. Accessed July 30, 2019. https://www.espn.com/espn/page2/story?page=jackson/060619_bias.

65. "What is Occam's Razor?" UCR Math. Accessed July 30, 2019. http://math.ucr.edu/home/baez/physics/General/occam.html.

66. "Of Rats, Rice, and Race: The Great Hanoi Rat Massacre, an Episode in French Colonial History." Freakonomics. Accessed July 30, 2019. http://www.freakonomics.com/media/vannrathunt.pdf.

67. "Operant conditioning." Wikipedia. Accessed July 30, 2019. https://en.wikipedia.org/wiki/Operant_conditioning.

68. *Nudge: Improving Decisions About Health, Wealth, and Happiness* by Richard H. Thaler, Cass R. Sunstein, page 4: https://www.goodreads.com/book/show/6359469-nudge

69. "Green defaults: Information presentation and pro ..." ScienceDirect.com. Accessed July 30, 2019. https://www.sciencedirect.com/science/article/abs/pii/S0272494407000758.

70. "The Hunger Games: Using hunger to promote ..." ScienceDirect.com. Accessed July 30, 2019. https://www.sciencedirect.com/science/article/pii/S0195666316308029.

71. "Nudging healthy food choices: a field experiment at the train ..." NCBI. Accessed July 30, 2019. https://www.ncbi.nlm.nih.gov/pubmed /26186924.

72. "Effects of group pressure upon the modification and ..." APA PsycNET. Accessed July 30, 2019. https://psycnet.apa.org/record/1952 -00803-001.

73. *Power Sleep: The Revolutionary Program That Prepares Your Mind for Peak Performance* by James B. Maas, page 16: https://www.goodreads.com /book/show/259777.Power_Sleep

74. "Natural selection." Understanding Evolution. Accessed July 30, 2019. https://evolution.berkeley.edu/evolibrary/article/evo_25.

75. *Mastery: The Keys to Success and Long-Term Fulfillment* by George Leonard, page 108: https://www.goodreads.com/book/show/18340786 -mastery

76. "Fight-or-flight response: Function of physiological changes." Wikipedia. Accessed July 30, 2019. https://en.wikipedia.org/wiki/Fight -or-flight_response.

77. "Stress potentiates decision biases: A stress ..." ScienceDirect.com. Accessed July 30, 2019. https://www.sciencedirect.com/science/article/pii /S2352289515300187.

78. "The Arrow of Time." Exactly What Is Time? Accessed July 30, 2019. http://www.exactlywhatistime.com/physics-of-time/the-arrow-of -time/.

79. "The Second Law of Thermodynamics." Edge.org. Accessed July 30, 2019. https://www.edge.org/response-detail/27023.

80. "Margin of Safety Definition and Examples used in Safety ..." OSTI. gov. Accessed July 30, 2019. https://www.osti.gov/servlets/purl/1134068.

81. *Antifragile: Things That Gain from Disorder* by Nassim Nicholas Taleb, page 3: https://www.goodreads.com/book/show/13530973-antifragile

82. *Antifragile: Things That Gain from Disorder* by Nassim Nicholas Taleb, page 159: https://www.goodreads.com/book/show/13530973-antifragile

83. "Threat and challenge: cognitive appraisal and stress ..." Academia. edu. Accessed July 30, 2019. https://www.academia.edu/11973248/Thre at_and_challenge_cognitive_appraisal_and_stress_responses_in_simula ted_trauma_resuscitations.

84. *Antifragile: Things That Gain from Disorder* by Nassim Nicholas Taleb, page 161: https://www.goodreads.com/book/show/13530973-antifragile

85. *The Principia: Mathematical Principles of Natural Philosophy* by Isaac Newton: https://www.goodreads.com/book/show/231083.The_Principia

86. *Homo Deus: A History of Tomorrow* by Yuval Noah Harari, page 83: https://www.goodreads.com/book/show/31138556-homo-deus

87. "Implementation Intentions and Effective Goal Pursuit." ResearchGate. Accessed July 30, 2019. https://www.researchgate.net /publication/37367645_Implementation_Intentions_and_Effective_Go al_Pursuit.

88. "Get Your Team to Do What It Says It's Going to Do." HBR. Accessed July 30, 2019. https://hbr.org/2014/05/get-your-team-to-do -what-it-says-its-going-to-do.

89. *Atomic Habits: An Easy & Proven Way to Build Good Habits & Break Bad Ones* by James Clear, page 15: https://www.goodreads.com/book/sh ow/40244063-atomic-habits

90. "Science and Statistics." Journal of the American Statistical Association. Accessed July 30, 2019. http://mkweb.bcgsc.ca/pointsofsigni ficance/img/Boxonmaths.pdf.

91. "The General Theory of Relativity." Accessed July 30, 2019. http://ion trap.umd.edu/wp-content/uploads/2016/01/WudkaGR-7.pdf.

92. *Sapiens: A Brief History of Humankind* by Yuval Noah Harari, page 288: https://www.goodreads.com/book/show/23198201-sapiens

93. "The Buffett Formula: Going to Bed Smarter Than When You Woke Up." Farnam Street. Accessed July 30, 2019. https://fs.blog/2013/05/the -buffett-formula/.

Printed in Great Britain
by Amazon